Playfulness

In Adult Life: Unlocking the Creativity Flow and Beyond

Insights from Six Decades of Playing, Teaching and Creating

Kefas Berlin

Playfulness In Adult Life
Unlocking the Creativity Flow and Beyond
- Insights from Six Decades of Playing, Teaching and Creating
Kefas Berlin Jannes

Copyright © 2025 by Kefas Berlin Jannes
All rights reserved
Publisher: BoD · Books on Demand, Östermalmstorg 1, 114 42 Stockholm,
Sverige, bod@bod.se
Print: Libri Plureos GmbH, Friedensallee 273, 22763 Hamburg, Tyskland

ISBN: 978-91-7969-052-6

Automated techniques used to analyse text and data in digital form for the purpose of
generating information, in accordance with Sections 15a, 15b, and 15c of the Copyright
Act (text and data mining), are prohibited.

Cover and Interior Design and Photos: Kefas Berlin Jannes

Thank you!

All the people I have met and had the privilege to talk to, to work and collaborate with, to play, practise, improvise and create with — friends, adults and children, artists and workshop participants. The collaborations, encounters, and the experience of them have taught me so much through their ways of being and doing. You know who you are. Thank you!

The persons that opened the doors to spaces where I could work and have those encounters and continue my path of investigation and creativity. You know who you are. Thank you!

My brother and my father for how the where, my mother for her trust and support of my choices, my children for how well they have raised me and taught me. Thank you!

Index

PART 1

Understanding Playfulness

The first element:

PART 2

Practicing Playfulness

PART 3

The child's play and its significance in Adult Life

PART 4

The Playfulness and Creativity Troubleshooting

Prelude

Playfulness in Adult Life:
Unlocking the Creativity Flow and Beyond

Dear Reader

Human beings are inherently creative.
It is through creation that we fully express what makes us human. Within each of us lies the ability to create—like a seed longing to be planted in fertile soil, where it can take root and flourish. And it is in this flourishing that we recognize ourselves, feel at home, and connect with our true power. We are all, in one way or another, artists.

The meaning of life is to live it and experience it—and everything that unfolds from that. **Meaning** is linked to wholeness. As long as you remain undivided and whole, the question of meaning does not arise.

Yet it is, however, the recurring inner condition of both the individual and humanity to find itself divided and un-whole. However, out of this outer and/or inner fragmentation and conflict arises the drive to reunite, to reconcile, to make whole —to create meaning, coherence, and a life that continues to grow. And, as the poet sang:

Ring the bells that still can ring
Forget your perfect offering
There is a crack, a crack in everything
That's how the light gets in   (L.Cohen)

By embracing that light in form of the ultimate inner freedom we have been given, and by choosing to approach life with playfulness and creativity—*which is always within our reach*—our existence becomes abundant: full of vitality and deep engagement. In doing so, the question of meaning becomes redundant. You are simply living your meaning.

When we start operating from our creative core with playfulness, we feel truly at home in our inner sensation of meaning. Meaning is about purpose, and every person, no matter where they are in life or what they do, is meant to **embrace** reality in some form—and as it is—and **create** something new from it. The essence of creativity cannot be separated from the essence of life's meaning.

As I earlier said, this creative capacity is with us from birth. It first manifests through play—through exploring the world and our own bodies, through social body play, rule-based play, fantasy play, and so on. And as we grow older, this innate play-drive continues in what we call creativity. *Essentially, however, creativity is nothing other than play.* The core of both play and creativity I call ***playfulness.***

Using the word playfulness may feel challenging, as we all associate it with different emotions and expressions. That is why I, in this book, will explore and define what I mean by playfulness—so that you can understand what I mean by playfulness.

In order to gain new insights into something you already knew what it was, it can be helpful to start completely from scratch, forgetting what you already knew in order to make space for new insights.

However, on the journey from childhood—perhaps not always a particularly playful one—to adulthood, most of us lose our sense of playfulness. And with it, creativity fades. The reasons for this may be deeply personal, yet they are also tied to the culture we live in and, more specifically, to the long years spent adapting to an educational system that shapes us. However, this book is not about how or why creativity disappears—there is already plenty of research on that. Instead, it explores how we can reclaim it. And we do so by understanding playfulness at its core and actively practicing its elements. Creativity then follows naturally—whether a second later or a day later.

Part 1: This part of the book offers an analysis of playfulness. It gives you a deeper understanding of what makes something playful and creative—the basic elements and their subgroups. Once you've grasped some of it, you'll be able to make use of the Troubleshooter in Part 4.

Part 2: This part offers practical exercises for playfulness— both for individuals and groups. Here, you'll dive into the elements of playfulness and find exercises that will significantly enhance your skills.

Part 3: This part delves into the role of childhood play and how its elements resurface in adulthood. It offers a way to understand essential aspects of life as an adult—in relation to well-being, social life, boundaries, rules, drama, creativity, joy, and more.

Part 4: The Troubleshooter. This may be the most important part, as it offers the actual keys to playfulness—and to the creativity that comes with it. You can turn to it when you find yourself missing playfulness or creativity—or even the sense of meaning in life—and need some understanding and insight, rather than more thinking. **Note:** Part 4 can't be used unless you've engaged with Part 1.

This book is a collection of experiences and insights that have emerged over four decades—in my pedagogical work with both children and adults and in my work as a musician and performing artist.

I hope that this book will offer you something valuable along your journey—in your life with others, with children and adults, with friends and lovers, in your professional life, in your encounters with yourself, and in your exploration of both the world and your inner being.

I hope it may inspire you in the creation of art and
in the creation of *life as art.*

*

Even as you read, you can begin practicing your playfulness through finding your own reading pace; sense when it is time to put the book down and when it feels right to continue. Do not become the dutiful student who diligently reads from cover to cover—instead, allow your impulsiveness to have space. Follow your curiosity. Take pauses. Let the text sink in. Let it also encourage you to pause from time to time and reflect on what the concepts and descriptions I present mean to you—how they are already present in your life and what you choose to do with them.

Why playfulness?

In an era marked by war, pain, depression, and a relentless tide of suicides, by greed and constant violations against nature, animals, and humanity, it may feel almost provocative to speak of playfulness. Is it really defensible to write about something as seemingly trivial as play? Isn't that an **insult** to the seriousness of the world? But what if playfulness is precisely what's missing? What if the world would be a different place if more of us had preserved the ability to play — to approach life with curiosity and openness, even as adults? There's a power in playfulness that fosters presence and compassion.

"Man only plays when he is, in the fullest sense of the word, human," Schiller wrote. But as digitization and AI take over increasing areas of our lives we risk losing what makes us human. True and profound connections, where we co-create and understand each other, are the last strongholds of our humanity. Even though we spend more time than ever on social media, research shows that feelings of loneliness are higher than ever. We may have more "friends" online, but these superficial interactions don't lead to the deep presence that creates genuine meaning. The digital world can keep us busy, but it doesn't keep us present — in our lives or our relationships. In a possible and likely quite near future, where digitalization and artificial intelligence dominate our daily lives, human connections, play, and **face-to-face interaction** become increasingly important elements. Perhaps these are precisely the elements that represent what is truly human. Perhaps it is through rediscovering the power of play in our relationships that we find our way back to what makes us whole as human beings.

"Homo Ludens" (Latin: the playing human) was coined by the Dutch historian and cultural philosopher Johan Huizinga in his book *Homo Ludens: A Study of the Play-Element in Culture* (1938). He emphasizes the central role that play (in a broad sense) has had and continues to have in human culture and civilization. It is time to highlight our species as **Homo Ludens** alongside our identity as **Homo Sapiens** (Latin: the knowing human).

Hans Kluge from the World Health Organization has labeled Mental Health Challenges as the "next pandemic" on the global horizon (2024), and the connection to our *growing isolation* is clear. We are distancing ourselves from what makes us human — from one another, and from playfulness. It's only in our encounters with the world, in real life, that playfulness can thrive. And at the same time, it is precisely playfulness that gives community its value and depth. It is both a tool and the very air that life itself breathes.

In an era of rapidly expanding AI technology, we are, quite literally, caught off guard. Groggy and astonished, we watch in awe the "intelligence" that AI represents. But AI itself is like an infant—equipped with an incredibly fast brain but without moral compass, compassion or life experience. Simply put, AI is intelligent but lacks the autonomy of action that integrates emotional intelligence.

By compassion, I mean the ability to sense and understand the needs of other living beings. By "the autonomy of action", the agency, I mean the realization and manifestation of thoughts, impulses, and intuitions.

It is precisely the union of compassion and agency that can save our planet. We are already intellectually intelligent enough. Paradoxically, it is our intelligence (our Homo *sapiens*) that is undermining our planet. As we all know, it is compassion that is lacking, along with a deep connection to what we are dealing with.

What is truly needed is **the sacred union** of three fundamental areas in human beings: *the awakening of thought and mind, the agency of will, and the compassionate, balancing intelligence of the heart.*

What I describe as playfulness is a synthesis of these three human capacities. Playfulness is something we can recognize in ourselves and others. It is also at the core of what psychologist *Mihály Csíkszentmihályi* referred to as ***Flow.*** When we are in Flow, we enter a creative state where we are not merely serving the task at hand — we are in connection with it. Information flows freely between everyone and everything involved. Both body and mind are highly alert but free from stress. The nervous system is balanced, and we expend no more energy than necessary. This, in turn, releases a cascade of beneficial hormones that enhance our mental and physical well-being.

These states of Flow are what the world needs. As humanity, we already know enough. Our challenge is not to acquire more knowledge but to manage the information we have in a way that cultivates and brings forth the best in every situation. This is not a question of smartness but of playfulness.

But I am hopeful.

Playfulness is not dependent on education, resources, or culture. It resides within all of us from the very beginning. But it is suffocated by norms and beliefs about what is "adult," "important," and "proper behavior." And it drowns in all the stress we subject ourselves to. The good news is that it's never too late. We can always rediscover our playfulness. And when we do, something wonderful happens — life unfolds in a new way. Our actions and thoughts ripple outward, affecting worlds far beyond our own.

Let's begin — with me... with you... with us.

Searching for playfulness

As a child I ran, climbed, played, and sang my way through the days, as if they were a tapestry of endless joy and motion. School imposed its limits, yes. But in the early years, there was still room for play — and so many songs. There was an endless stream of stories,  fairy tales, legends, and myths—from Europe and Scandinavia to India, the Middle East, and Greece. All of Western history unfolded like a patchwork quilt of explorers, scientists, heroes, thinkers, musicians, authors and warriors. My soul was filled with images, and they would remain, transform, grow, and constantly bear new fruits.

My parents emerged from the darkness of the Second World War. My father from Nazi-occupied Copenhagen, and my mother from the utterly bombed-out ruins of Hamburg. It was, quite simply, a matter of survival—for both moral and practical reasons—to piece together one fragment after another, to create something useful out of almost nothing.

But both my father and mother were deeply creative in the sense that, whatever they had in their hands, they could turn it into something entirely new—something that hadn't existed before, and something that held meaning for them.

Among their parents and extended family were artists and artisans, inventors, primary school teachers, and photographers. To be creative was part of life. And both their lives would go on to be shaped by that very spirit: the spirit of creating something new—and, in their eyes, beautiful—out of anything at all: whether as an exhibition designer, a craftsperson, or a teacher. I was shaped by my parents and the culture they passed down

For me it was the moving, the playing and the singing that nurtured and carried me, giving life its direction. Far beyond any notion of mere pastime, play was, for me, a way of being in the world — perhaps even surviving it. I was what one might call a sensitive nature, and life poured into me with such intensity that I had to process it, reshape it, and create something new from it.

Whatever a person receives, they must in some way process—like the bread we chew, swallow, digest, and process, which then becomes energy. What is left must be expelled. So too must the soul metabolize all it encounters. For me, play became this metabolism of the soul — a vital process, as organic as a heartbeat.

The singing and the movement, the playing and the joy — they were driven by something within, something that could neither be taught nor explained, only lived. Through them, I grew into life, like a tree rooting itself and sending out shoots, ever onward. I was, at once, deeply introverted and wild and untamed on the outside. Studying and practicing did not come naturally to me. Play, however — that was my way of approaching the world.

Play harbours no hidden agenda of utility. And yet, it is undeniably useful — it nurtures learning and development. We all know this, but we must begin to take it more seriously. Play is vital, yet all too often it is dismissed as a luxury, rather than recognized as essential. We are well aware that play fuels creativity, connection, learning, and even healing — and yet we continue to set it aside in favour of 'serious' work or productivity. True play arises from within, guided by motives — conscious or unconscious — unique to the individual. To channel what longs to be play into a pedagogical exercise risks diluting its twin essence: presence and interaction. And without that essence, little else retains much worth, no matter how polished or refined it may seem.

This same playful attitude accompanied me in music. I played an instrument for as long as the joy remained, as long as inspiration stayed by my side — never to become skilled. This approach led me to many instruments, and many sounds, and perhaps it was this openness that laid the foundation for my love of diversity. Like a juggler delighting in adding more and more balls. The more, the merrier, the more thrilling to keep them aloft. My starting point was never, *"This is what I can do, and nothing more."* It was always, *"What is this I do not yet know? What will it take to master it?"* And this, too, is the essence of play — a resounding *yes* to the world.

After school, I considered becoming an actor, a composer or a dancer. That would come to pass later on, but at the time, as a 20-year-old, life led me elsewhere — to a residential home and school for children with severe autism. It was a place and a group of people I felt at home with, having grown up with a brother who was severely autistic, with whom I'd always shared a strong bond and deep sense of connection. I had no formal training and no particular method to draw upon. But I carried with me a quiet confidence in simply being myself — a confidence that stemmed from my sense of playfulness. A playfulness that carried a belief: *"I'll figure something out, moment by moment."* And that mindset took me far.

But these children did not play.

Play is a sign of well-being.
It signals that one is sufficiently fed, warm, and safe in oneself. This is true for animals and humans.

So, what use was my playfulness in the face of their anxiety, when they did not even know where in the world they themselves belonged? I remember my supervisor, Miss Hilde Barfoot appreciated my playfulness with the children and recognised that there was something good in it for them.

What was it she noticed? I was present with them. In fact, mentally, I was present within them. Outwardly, they appeared as a tangle of baffling "behaviours." What was I supposed to do with that? Had I stayed focused on their outward behaviours, it wouldn't have led anywhere. But to me, their inner world wasn't a confusing mess. It was accessible — if I could look past the surface, beyond the "behaviours," and reach for what lay underneath.

That connection became the starting point for anything meaningful we could accomplish together. And we did accomplish things. Perhaps that's what Miss Barfoot meant by playfulness.

Presence — Connection — Interaction in motion
This became my way of reaching them, and theirs of reaching me.

After a couple of years, Miss Barfoot gave me a new task: to work musically with each of the children individually. I had no method, no textbook to lean on. All I had was my presence, my playfulness. And through that, step by step, we developed a form of music-making entirely on *their* terms. It wasn't music education — it was musical interaction and a healing companionship.

Life took me further — to pedagogical education, music- and dance trainings and to working with other children and adults. The materials for my tools remained the same: movement, play, dance, music, song, and theatre. And always, my core tool was the same: playfulness — and through it, creativity.

Eventually, I met Werner Kuhfuß: a thinker, therapeutic educator, play therapist, course leader, and author devoted to the nature of play. His sharp insights into the essence of play became a key for me. He showed me how play could become a field of discovery — not just for children, but for adults too. How it opens doors to ourselves, to group dynamics, to life itself.

Through encounters with thousands of people — children and adults — at schools, open workshops, and training centres, and through artistic work on stage and with music, I learned to ask questions about playfulness and creativity: ***What makes it work? What happens when it doesn't? What's missing? And what does it really mean for play to work?***

These questions and the answers that emerged, I also took with me into daily life, into relationships, into parenting, into interaction with nature, animals, into everyday tasks and, yes, even to the washing-up brush.

I wanted to understand what made a situation playful, creative, and optimal — what it was that brought out the best and most growth-promoting qualities from both the situation and its participants.

I discovered that three elements are always present when playfulness arises: ***interaction, presence, and a dynamic flow***.

Over time, I came to see that these principles apply not only to playfulness but to all creative endeavors — and to life itself. In playfulness lies a force, a generative energy that we all carry within us. And it is in this force that we find our *yes* to life.

The Theatre Studio

Before I delve into describing play and playfulness, their building blocks and how they can be practiced, I would like to briefly share my time at Teaterstudion Vårdinge By, part of the Folk High School Vårdinge By.

It was a period of deep immersion in the very themes this book explores. It was also there that many of the seeds were sown for the exercises I describe later in the book.

To sketch the background roughly:
for nearly twenty years, I had worked in pedagogy, studied dance and music, and spent a great deal of time on stage before

being employed as an actor at *Teater Sláva*, a professional Free Theatre on the outskirts of Stockholm.

> *At the heart of their theatrical explorations and productions was a focus on the possibilities of movement and the voice, and an intense core of presence and drama.* **Theatre Sláva** *had historical influences from the Polish theatre group Gardzienice and the theatrical work of Jerzy Grotowski.*

After a year as an actor, I was also offered a position at *Vårdinge By Folk High School,* on the theatre programme. I worked there alongside my role at Teater Slava.

What I'm about to describe was training designed specifically for the performing arts. Yet, although it was aimed at performers, it was here that my understanding of playfulness and creativity deepened significantly. These were ideas that had first taken root some 20 years earlier and would continue to evolve long after my time at the Theatre Studio. Between 1999 and 2009, I had the privilege of working as a teacher for the actor students. The programme was a full-time, one-year course delivered on-site. "The Theatre Studio Vårdinge By". From 2002 to 2009, I was leading the programme and serving as its principal teacher in Physical Actors training; Voice and Movement, Acrobatics, Contact Improvisation, Bogart´s Viewpoints, Laban Technique, Creativity and as their Director.

The focus was entirely on *"liberating the possibilities of the voice, freeing movement expression, and unlocking creativity."* Thus voice, movement, and creativity were at the core, rather than productions of dramatic works.

The skills of **Presence** and **Interaction** are essential to all forms of stage art, including dance, theatre, music, and performance. For this reason, significant and daily time was devoted to practicing and training these two abilities. As they are *interdependent,* they were always practised in an integrated manner.

To understand the students' strengths and weaknesses in their interactions, I needed to analyze how they approached the interaction tasks and exercises. Based on my observations, I could then develop appropriate exercises to support their growth in this area. This led me to my first deeper understanding of **Interaction**.

I divided the process of Interaction into three *phases*:

Input—Resonance—Output

It based on the observation that students tended to *struggle in one phase more than the others.*

- **Input** refers to the inflow of information from fellow performers, props, lighting, the audience, the room, time, and everything else present in the moment.

- **Resonance** is what happens "beneath the surface" — how the incoming information resonates within the performer, where it lands, and how it is processed.

- **Output** is the impulse that arises from the resonance and manifests as an action.

The ideal state (inspired by Polish director and teacher Jerzy Grotowski as well as Italian/Danish Eugenio Barba) was to *eliminate the time gap between input and output while still incorporating resonance.*

> *The aim was for the performer to exist in* **simultaneity** *with fellow performers and everything else present in the space and moment. Any delay between input and output disrupts the dynamic-dramatic-musical flow of time. Actors, dancers, and musicians should function as* **one body** *— ideally, being one with everything else in the room and the moment.*

> *A time gap, even if only a second long, represents* **an absence***. Absence is the opposite of presence. In a dancing pair, such a gap can be detrimental; for actors, it disrupts the dramatic flow; for a musical ensemble, it diminishes the audience's musical experience.*

The exercises therefore had to be designed with this specific goal in mind: to *eliminate the time gap* between an input and the output it triggered. In other words, a temporal unity where input and output ideally *become one.* This creates an enhanced interaction and *mutuality* between everything and everyone present on stage, as well as the influences brought by the audience and the unique conditions of the day. An exceptionally ambitious objective!

Students typically exhibited either a **sluggishness or a slowing down** in their input *or* output, depending on their personality. Therefore, I developed exercises that targeted one *or* the other weakness specifically.

Resonance was also a focus of practice. This involved deeply *absorbing and integrating an impression* before transforming it into expression. Figuratively speaking: like one great, deep breath drawn before the next release. The impression could be someone else's movement, a tone, a piece of music, a colour, a line of poetry, and so on. The key to the exercise was: *fading into the impression and allowing it to settle within you, integrating it before releasing it as an action. One could say: a **re-action,** emerging from a deep digestion, but still a reaction, not an action.*

Of course, for the sake of energy and the desire to create, it was important to strike a *balance* between focusing on what needed practice and focusing on what was already there. Addressing both shortcomings and what flows freely and works.

During these years, I gained a profound understanding of **Interaction**, and my personal journey towards deeper **Presence** also evolved.

> *In this context, I would also like to mention the director **Anne Bogart** and her **"9 Viewpoints"** model (Bogart/Landau, 2005), which has been — and remains — an excellent tool for training presence and interaction, generating artistic material, and revitalising work that has fallen into stagnation. This approach involves viewing the stage's Time- and Space-elements from nine different **Viewpoints**, limiting one's field of focus in order to **heighten**

*presence in a particular element — such as **duration, tempo, repetition, kinestetic respons, gesture, spatial relationships**, **architecture, topography and shape.***

Presence training was a constant. Presence is at the foundation of everything; through it, one can cultivate interaction. Interaction can, in turn, motivate and nourish presence, just as it can awaken and elevate presence. In any case, one must be present and decisive in choosing what to focus on and what action to take.

Presence training could be continuously refined — there is, in fact, no limit to the power of presence. The exercises were always designed to challenge presence to the very edge of its capacity.

Over time, the students noticed that they experienced more through their senses. Their senses, like their attention, were opened and sharpened through the interactive presence exercises, and that is a natural consequence of such exercises. The world that the senses **reveal** became an ever-growing source of inspiration.

Energy and Presence

Energy is a fundamental parameter in stage performance. Just as energy is required for **mental presence**, one may also discover that presence itself (which, of course, depends on a *conscious decision* to be present) *generates energy.* It is easy to conclude that **presence and energy exist in a reciprocal relationship** — a principle widely used by many performing artists and within sports.

Presence generates **both mental and biological energy**. This is linked to the relationship between sensory stimulation, movement, stress hormones, and increased metabolism. The key difference between a **stressful or life-threatening situation** and a **stage performance** is that in the latter, you make a conscious choice. You decide that **something specific must be of utmost importance**, and that is where you place your presence — as if it were a matter of life and death.

For example: you decide that your opponent's hand is of utmost importance and requires your full attention. It becomes crucial that you examine and understand everything there is to know about this hand, you tell yourself. Nothing else holds value at that moment—only the hand. (The audience's attention and presence will, in proportion to your own, be drawn to your opponent's hand.) The key to this is the markedly heightened presence. The interaction that then arises between you and your opponent will be saturated with presence.

My research at Teaterstudion — as well as my personal artistic practice, both before and after that period — forms the foundation for the descriptions, exercises, and reflections that follow. I am forever grateful for the efforts of my students and workshop participants, both before, after, and during the Theatre Studio years.

*

However, what I am about to describe is **not** limited to stage performers. It is intended for **anyone** who wishes to cultivate greater playfulness and creativity in all aspects of life.

PART 1

understanding Playfulness

To grow into life

Play is the way through which we, as human beings, grow into life — the optimal way. The very best way. I can think of no better expression for what happens when we *enter a state of play,* something essential to every person's life: ***to grow into life!***

To grow into life means integrating the many facets of our physical, emotional and spiritual existence into a harmonious, organic whole.

But what does an ***organic whole*** entail?
For something to function as a whole, the internal communication within the whole must flow freely and efficiently. Each individual or organism is composed of smaller parts, yet also belongs to a greater whole. Health emerges when the internal communication within the organism and the external communication with the environment are in balance. This can manifest in the relationship between a person and nature, work, other people, the food we eat, the air we breathe, or the impressions we absorb through our senses.

When communication breaks — internally or externally — the flow within the whole is disrupted. An organism cannot function when a part of it is cut off from interaction. When the whole is disturbed, dis-ease emerges — a state of dis-integration.

A clear example is cancer. Simply put, cells that no longer cooperate with the body as a whole but grow unchecked place a burden on the organism until it collapses. Similarly, society can be filled with elements that fail to contribute to the whole, instead becoming a strain. The internal communication and the organic interaction is broken.

Nature — and our bodies, as part of it — carries an inherent playfulness. As long as this flow remains undisturbed, nature handles its processes with creativity and adaptive playfulness. But when disruptions become too numerous or too intense, even nature reaches its limits. If we wish to support healing — whether in nature or within ourselves — it involves creating space and time for playfulness to resurface.

To be in a state of playfulness or flow is to allow **presence, interaction, and dynamics** to generate the flow necessary for a functioning organic whole. It is through playfulness that we craft *a personal and integrated wholeness.*

But growing into life is not about outward expansion — about acquiring more, multiplying, or becoming greater. It is about inward growth, about creating and manifesting the wholeness we carry within ourselves as individuals.

We are born as a whole, a vibrating being filled with sensations and experiences. At the very beginning of our lives, we are one with everything that is and everything that happens. We have no understanding yet, no thoughts or concepts— everything simply is. All sensory impressions and emotional moods flow into us, causing our body to react and move with whatever comes in. But with each passing day, the need to grasp the world, to interact with its components and beings, awakens. Step by step, we begin to understand, orient ourselves, and form a personal relationship with it.

Our experiences expand in scope and become differentiated. This is where play comes in. ***The state of play becomes our tool in this process.*** It is through play that we grow into ourselves, feel ourselves and sense the world. It is through play we come to know both ourselves and the world.

Through being in play, we learn to regulate and handle our bodies, our senses, and our emotions. We grow into our inner world and become creators within it. Play serves as a bridge between our internal spaces and the external world. It forges new connections, new wholes, and helps us grow into life as integrated, harmonious individuals.

To understand ***playfulness*** is vital. Playfulness is not about ***what*** we do but ***how we do it.*** It is an approach that can be cultivated through practice and awareness.

Playfulness consists of three essential elements:

presence   *interaction*

dynamics

In this book, we will explore what these three elements mean and entail. We will look at how we can awaken these abilities. Through practice, we can develop our capacity for playfulness and, in turn, approach life in a deeper and more meaningful way —even in times of difficulty.

Play and Playfulness

Over the years, I began to discover play in situations that weren't explicitly called play but still had a playful quality. It wasn't the degree of joy or humor that determined this; it was playful, even though it wasn't play in the traditional sense. But what was it?

I realized the importance of **distinguishing between the concepts of play and playfulness.** They are closely intertwined, yet have distinct characteristics. Understanding the difference between them is something I consider important. Distinguishing play as *a phenomenon* from playfulness as *an ability* is an important step towards understanding playfulness on a deeper level. When I reach that point, playfulness becomes something increasingly tangible and graspable—something not confined to resembling play or to everything we associate with play.

*This deeper understanding allows us to see how playfulness can permeate everything we do. It is then that playfulness elevates life, bringing a richness it has never known before. It is then that life itself can become art. **For art, creativity and playfulness are one and the same.***

When something is playful, it means that an activity is infused with creativity. Playfulness is the essence of a functioning play or creativity — its vitality. Play is the form, while playfulness is the essence that brings play to life and fills it with energy.

Play is what is done
— the form of a certain activity.
Playfulness is how it is done
— the life force within the form of play.

The insight into this distinction is central. Playfulness is a quality that can permeate any activity, regardless of its outward form. Playfulness is not limited to what we typically consider play. It's more about the approach you take to what you're doing. Research into play shows that this is an innate trait in humans — a vital way of learning and developing, a way of growing into the world.

> *Developmental psychology takes it a step further:*
> *Play (i.e. playfulness) has been crucial to human survival and development. It is a means of adaptation, where the individual learns and grows without losing their integrity. Those who lack this ability to play may find themselves excluded. This pattern is seen in both mammals and hunter-gatherer cultures.*

In play research, the word play is used for both specific games and a playful way of acquiring knowledge. However, to create playfulness in adult life, we must free ourselves from the notion that playfulness and play are the same thing. Otherwise, we risk thinking that playfulness is about being childish, silly, or humorous. Or as the 8-year-old put it: *"They (adults) don't really play. When they play, they pretend to play!"*

We can learn from small children. When they are undisturbed and have the time they need, they are completely present in what we call play. They explore how to interact with someone or something in a meaningful way. By meaningful, I don't mean "useful." Some researchers consider the "uselessness" of play to be one of its primary characteristics. This does not mean that play lacks value. On the contrary, it is invaluable for emotional, social, cognitive, and motor development. But the inner motivation that drives play is not about achieving something useful. The one who plays is not preoccupied with thoughts of utility but rather with the satisfaction found in the act of playing itself, in the here and now.

Play has no goal aimed at the future; its significance is found in the present. When the player starts to aim their focus toward the future, playfulness is lost. Here lies the paradox of play: It is crucial for the *future* development of the individual and society, yet it is entirely rooted in and focused on the *here and now*.

In order to reclaim playfulness, we need, as is often said, *to become like children*—not outwardly, but inwardly. It is playfulness, rather than specific games, that drives a child's development. A game without playfulness lacks its essence, while playfulness, without being a specific game, still fosters development.

Playfulness always creates its own form in which to live—just as a healthy river creates its own shapes as it flows through the landscape. It is not the river-bed that creates the shape of the rivers path. The river itself possesses these shape-creating forces. The form and path of the river through the landscape are shaped by the water's meeting and interaction with what the landscape offers: mountains, forests, and meadows.

And so it is with playfulness.

Play

It became clear to me that, unlike playfulness, play concerns the very form of an activity. Play research expresses this as follows:

> *Play is a specific activity that is bounded both in time and space. It has agreed-upon rules and conditions that are either set in advance or developed during the course of the play. The form and structure are central.*

Rules, along with the boundaries of space and time, help create a zone of safety where the player can move freely. Within this zone, she can "stretch her limits," both physically and in her imagination.

Boundaries in the form of rules can be stretched, but not broken. Play can evolve in terms of rules, direction, and content, but there is always a stable foundation. This foundation can be a desire to discover, a desire to move, a desire to play, a desire for belonging — or something else. The foundation may vary between participants, but without this foundation, the player will feel the absence and sense the need to find it. Perhaps not consciously or expressed, but as a feeling. *When this simple, primary foundation is missing, the structure becomes unstable. And then non-play elements such as motivation for victory, power, or status begin to creep in.*

Each participant feels the need for *a personal and genuine motive to engage in the play.* Without such a motive, and as mentioned, multiple motives can coexist within the same play, the play loses its inherent meaning. This meaning is hard to capture in words but can definitely be felt. When play loses its *self-motivating foundation,* it can transform into something else — a struggle or competition where compassion and empathy often lose their place.

In summary: ***Play needs to be self-motivated.*** When it comes to playing with others, each participant's motives must coexist and form a shared foundation. The walls and roof of play are built from agreed-upon or unwritten rules, forms, and structures. These create a *safety net* that allows participants to feel secure and free in their fantasies and movements. Without a 'safe space' for play to unfold, they will struggle to find a *substitute*. As a result, non-play elements such as status, power, or a focus on winning will take over—and that marks the end of the play.

As adults, we must accept that life is not a game in the traditional sense. But that doesn't mean we cannot live playfully. As long as we lack playfulness, we will chase—after money, power, love—believing that these must be conquered. The most important things in life, the ones that give meaning, are not things we need to fight for. They are already there, hidden but alive, like a seed beneath the earth.
What we need is to nourish this seed, to revive the art of playfulness. Through it, the most important things in life can begin to bloom.

Playfulness is not about winning the world, but about living in it and with it—a way of letting life itself win through us.

Playfulness

Play is about what is done—it is the form of an activity. Playfulness is about how it is done—it is the life within the form.

Play = Form
Playfulness = Life

Playfulness is not tied to any specific activity. It can be present in play, but just as easily in dancing, conversation, walking in nature, singing, artistic creation—or in everyday tasks like brushing your teeth, painting a wall, or designing a workspace. It is a quality of approach, a particular way of relating to what is at hand.

By "material," I mean the facts, circumstances, or elements we are faced with—what reality presents to us. This material can take countless forms: something physical like wood, metal, colour, the voice, tone, or the body itself. It might also be less tangible—such as someone's actions or expressions, spoken or unspoken rules of interaction, or even how we structure time in studies, work, teaching, or parenting.

Ideas, thoughts, impulses, and emotions are also part of this material. So are conversations, creative processes, exploration, and research—provided we choose to engage with them as such.

To be playful is to meet the material with
inner freedom, curiosity, and creativity.
It is to approach life not as a set of constraints
but as a space of possibility.

To be playful is to let yourself be surprised by what is already there, to see the familiar with fresh eyes, and to respond openly—rather than imposing a predetermined outcome.

Playfulness invites a dialogue with the material. It means listening to what it "says," allowing it to shape the interaction without centering yourself as the sole driver. In this ebb and flow between expression and reception, between doing and noticing, new paths emerge.

Although we often recognize playfulness from the act of play, my focus here is on playfulness as a distinct quality—one that transcends play itself. It is a way of being that can permeate teaching, mentoring, artistic activities, relationships, or even the mundane rhythms of daily life.

When we begin to understand playfulness as something independent of play, we gain the ability to nurture it intentionally and apply it across all areas of life, both large and small.

For many adults, especially in a world that prizes seriousness and utility, playfulness may feel remote, even frivolous. *Yet, there is no contradiction between playfulness and seriousness.* Realizing this has been one of my most valuable insights.

The Optimal State

Playfulness creates an optimal state. Whether it is learning, creating, interacting, or even engaging in play itself, playfulness enhances each situation and brings it closer to its full potential.

By "optimal," I mean that *a playful approach deepens the experience and elevates what is possible within a given moment.* A conversation reaches its fullest expression when approached playfully; the same goes for creative or learning processes.

However, playfulness cannot be manufactured through sheer willpower. It is easily constrained by *personal expectations or assumptions.* For example, if I equate playfulness with needing to be funny, fast-paced, or entertaining, these expectations might block the natural flow of playfulness.

Interestingly, there is no real opposition between playfulness and fun—but true playfulness cannot be reduced to a desire for fun, creativity, or flow. Paradoxically, if we chase these outcomes too hard, we often miss the doorway into playfulness itself.

Playfulness is free from
destinations
It carries no agenda,
yet resonates with meaning
Within its flow,
there is no striving for
an end,
only the wonder
of what emerges
now,
and now,
and now

The three core elements of playfulness

To foster playfulness, you must first recognize and embrace three essential elements, which I will now describe.

I've observed that when something is playful, it contains an element of **presence, interaction, and dynamics**. I've also seen that if any of these elements are missing, playfulness vanishes.

Moreover, I've noticed that these elements support each other mutually. One element needs the other two to be truly strong.

The first element:

Presence

Presence is the ability to be in a state of awake, attentive, conscious, and unreserved experience of what exists here and now. To be present is simply to *be*—but at the same time, to be aware of what I have chosen to be present in.

Doing stands in contrast to *being.* However, we can **be** in our doing, just as we can allow what we **do** to be an expression of who or what we **are** at that moment. The activity in which we feel most at home or most at ease is the one where we can fully be who we are at that time.

the optimal state:

*To do what one is,
so that one can fully be
what one is
in the act of doing.*

What playfulness does is expand and develop aspects of ourselves we did not know existed. In every playful moment of our lives, qualities that have lain dormant are awakened— qualities that belong to our fundamental being.

It seems, however, that as human beings, *we cannot be present without having an experience*—in other words, without our consciousness being filled with something *beyond ourselves.* We need to experience in order to be present. Experience, however, is not the same as presence. Presence is greater and beyond all content, yet the degree of presence is dependent on how much I can surrender to an experience.

What we experience, we usually perceive as real. The reality I experience here and now is the reality I am capable of engaging with, and my ability to engage with it is proportional to how present I am.

Through my presence, I can *choose my approach* to reality: to change it; to create with it.

Presence ensures that I am not entirely conditioned *by* reality, but that I can also condition it. My ability to handle reality depends on my presence.

If I am only *half-heartedly* present, reality slips through my fingers—it is not easy to grasp what is drifting away.

My presence conditions my awareness of the reality I stand in right now.

> *Later in the book, I will delve into the obstacles and challenges that hinder or complicate presence.*

Presence Requires:

1. *Focus*

A clear decision on what to focus on, where or in what you should place your presence, and the ability to maintain it until a new decision is made.

2. *Inner Silence*

Quieting disruptive inner commentary, judgments, conclusions, and overthinking. Inner silence is achieved through cultivating a deeper and stronger focus.

Interlude:
the war against presence

A clear and tangible feature of our society today—and one that will likely remain so for a long time to come—is the ongoing battle for our attention. Private and, above all, commercial interests compete to capture our focus through the countless digital platforms available. Psychological and neurological expertise has been developed to bind our presence and attention to their products as effectively as possible. This is a competition that is accelerating in pace, sensory stimulation, suggestion, and the number of cuts per minute.

Our brains are not primarily designed to focus but rather to scan reality. This ability, science tells us, was key to our survival on the savannah, and neither our brain nor our DNA has changed significantly since then.

However, the brain has an incredible capacity to adapt to the ever-increasing influx of information. Tolerance levels rise, meaning the amount of information per second must escalate to capture our attention and keep our minds engaged. Physiologically, this is described as "more must happen" for a sufficient amount of dopamine to be released.

Dopamine is a neurotransmitter that, together with dopamine receptors, allows us to be present and focused. Studies have shown that the downside of this rising information overload is cognitive fatigue—the brain becomes drained and struggles to maintain focus. When engaging with social media, we do not need to exercise our "presence muscle"—our ability to focus. The platform and the content provider do the "work." As a result, our "presence muscle" weakens.

Research indicates that people—children, adolescents, and adults alike—are finding it increasingly difficult to concentrate. A study from the University of California, Irvine, examined how long it takes before we shift our attention from one task to another. The time has decreased from 150 seconds in 2004 to 47 seconds today (2024) before our focus broken.

From the perspective of this book, we can say that playfulness and creativity are gasping for air amid this battle for our presence. And this is precisely what research is showing: a significant decline in children's play.

It's not just about the time spent on social media, but also about the fact that, once the phone is put aside, the outside world seems less engaging. What it truly comes down to is that the brain, deprived of dopamine, is too exhausted to be present.

But presence is what elevates reality into something that is, in one way or another, always engaging. That's all there is to it. Presence is crucial for connecting with reality and being able to interact with it. Therefore, we can say that there is a war against something fundamentally human within us: playfulness and creativity.

These observations are supported by a growing body of interdisciplinary research across neuroscience, psychology, and pedagogy. Scholars such as Johann Hari (2022) and Manfred Spitzer (2012) have highlighted the neurological costs of an overstimulated digital environment, linking it to rising issues of attention deficits and diminished creative capacities. In this context, presence is not merely a psychological state but a prerequisite for engaging creatively with the world. The erosion of this ability undermines fundamental human faculties, echoing the warnings of thinkers such as Winnicott and

Csikszentmihalyi, who each emphasized the need for a focused presence in fostering play, creativity, and well-being.

This analysis calls for a re-examination of how modern life interfaces with our biological needs and a renewed commitment to creating environments where presence—and thus playfulness—can thrive.

The second element:

Interaction

Interaction refers to what can arise between you and someone else, between you and a group of people you are leading or teaching, or between you and something. Interaction depends primarily on mental presence and, in most cases, physical presence as well. It occurs when there is both connection and reciprocity. For interaction to deepen and evolve, "resonance" is required (explained below).

Interaction can also be observed in a chemist's laboratory or a kitchen. When you mix two substances and perhaps apply heat, the contents of the test tube or saucepan begin to respond to your actions. You observe what happens, adjust your approach, and make decisions — lowering the heat or adding a touch of pepper. In this process, information, in the form of actions or scents, flows back and forth between you and the recipient/sender.

When working with materials, as a chef or sculptor might, the responses from your counterpart are relentless and unforgiving. They respond according to their nature, much like how the floor and gravity confront and challenge the dancer. In such situations, it becomes *your responsibility to embody the internal flexibility* and freedom needed to adapt to what is offered.

This is about cultivating your inner ability to make free choices — because playfulness cannot thrive without a free and open approach.

Reciprocity with the material arises as you act, listen, respond, listen again, and respond further. The sequence begins with your action but quickly turns into a chain of *re-actions* to the responses you receive from the material. *This is when interaction truly comes to life.*

As the director tells the actor: stop acting and start reacting!
Actions become answers to answers
— or better yet, offerings in response to offerings, as new offerings.

Interaction with another living being is more complex. Your counterpart has their own will, carries their desires, and may, like you, not always be fully present, flexible, connected, or reciprocal. Their responses may not be as immediate or obvious as when there's too much pepper in a soup.

Now, I will examine the skill of interaction in more detail and describe what it needs to develop into an increasingly robust and effective ability.

Interaction Requires:

1. Contact and Acceptance

2. Reciprocity

3. Resonance

- Contact and acceptance

The foundation of all interaction lies in establishing and maintaining contact. This contact is nourished by two fundamental qualities:

Flexibility and Adaptability—The ability to follow and respond with acceptance to both external initiatives and impulses as well as those arising from within.

Initiative—The ability to take action, realize inner impulses, and manifest one's will.

To keep contact alive, thereby enabling interaction, one must alternate between the poles of **leading** and **following**.
These poles rest upon two essential qualities: **will** and **willingness**.

Contact dissipates if the balance is lost — where one exclusively leads or follows. This is akin to a lung collapsing when it only exhales or bursting when it only inhales.

When contact falters, it can often be traced to two causes:

- *A failure to take the initiative required by the situation at that specific time.*

- *A lack of attentiveness or adaptability to perceive and integrate the information presented, which is essential for an appropriate response.*

This dynamic is particularly evident in artistic processes. Artists experiencing a "creative drought" may feel trapped in the belief that they must invent and create everything themselves. They might assume that they must always be productive and original. Such a mindset often overlooks, or never grasps, the importance of listening — not just to oneself but also to the materials at hand.

Listening forms the bedrock of all art and communication.
It is not limited to living beings; even materials like clay, wood, stone, paint, and sound have something to convey. Artistic creation, at its core, is a dialogue — a form of interaction with the material. Similarly, playfulness is always a form of communication, always in touch with reality.

To be in contact requires Acceptance

Being and remaining in contact is challenging because it demands an unreserved "Yes!" To affirm and embrace what comes — whether from external sources or within oneself — is an art that often requires great trust and personal surrender.

To be present and in contact, I must first accept what is before trying to understand or categorize it. Delaying acceptance until I have "figured it out" risks losing the connection entirely. Overthinking can make me miss the moment. An unreserved "Yes!" requires faith that I will be able to handle whatever arises — or that the capacity to manage it will emerge in the encounter itself.

Leaping in without "testing the waters" can be crucial. Our judgments of what is "hot" or "cold" — of what is desirable or undesirable — can otherwise obstruct connection and create resistance. By saying Yes! to whatever arises, we reduce this selectivity and open ourselves to a broader perception of reality.

But must I always say Yes?

No, there are times when a No is necessary. However, the key lies in how that No is communicated. A No can be expressed in a way that preserves connection. Instead of blocking, I can redirect the energy toward affirming something else.

> *Consider the principle of Aikido: the practitioner meets the force of an attack by absorbing it and redirecting it in a new direction, rather than blocking it outright. Confronting aggression with counter-aggression risks severing the connection and escalating the conflict. By redirecting the energy, contact is maintained, the interaction can continue, and creative solutions remain possible.*

Thus, saying No is not about rejecting or shutting down. It is often about shifting focus or channeling energy. Redirect the moment. This approach preserves the connection.

Outer stop, Inner flow

In Chinese dance theatre, or Jing Ju, there is a saying: *"Outer stop, inside no stop!"*

This means that even if the outer movement halts, the inner movement — attention and presence — must remain uninterrupted.

The same principle is practiced in music, particularly in phrasing. Melodies are divided into phrases, and it is the musician's sensitivity that determines their length. A musical piece does not end when the musician pauses to breathe or when the instrument falls silent. No, presence and attention must remain constant, in unbroken flow, until the piece concludes. *"Outer stop, inside no stop!"*

Why is the Yes so important?

Affirmation and embrace forms the foundation of connection. Without it, I lose the ability to engage with what is given — the object, the situation, or the other person. By saying YES, I accept what is, which is a prerequisite for using, transforming, and playing with it.

This principle is the core of all improvisational performance art: saying YES to what happens, accepting it, and then using it in the act of creation. This is expressed in the mantra: *"Never say No, but Yes, and...!"*

Blocking or stopping impulses leads to stagnation.

With a YES, contact is preserved, and with it, playfulness is made possible. Playfulness depends on my willingness to keep the connection alive, no matter the situation. It requires me to see each moment as an opportunity to interact and create — *to say Yes, to embrace, affirm, and "make the most of" whatever comes my way.*

- Reciprocity

Communication and interaction, on any level, require Reciprocity. For young children, this means getting accustomed to the idea of "taking turns." Initially, this concept is puzzling to them. Why should I share my time or the thing I'm holding in my hand? Why shouldn't I exert my strength when I am the strongest of the two? As children grow older, this dynamic becomes more complex. Being the fastest, the strongest, or the smartest can become loaded metrics celebrated in our culture, particularly in schools, both socially and in relation to grading systems. However, when the foundational values of play are replaced by such competition-laden values, *playfulness dies.* No play survives this shift.

Animals

How do animals behave when they play? Studies of animal play (e.g., Bekoff 1995; 2001; 2007) show that individuals who are stronger, faster, or higher ranked often "downgrade" their advantages and privileges. This is known as ***self-handicapping***. By self-handicapping, the stronger, faster, or higher-ranked individual brings themselves down to the same level as the one they are playing with. But why would the stronger individual handicap themselves? The answer is simple: ***for the play to continue.*** If the play turns into a competition or a display of advantages over others, it loses its playful nature and dies.

At the core, everyone wants to play. Animal play typically lacks the element of *"playing to win something."* They simply play until they are exhausted or hungry. Individuals who cannot maintain this mindset are ignored. Those who break this fundamental rule — who cannot participate in the play — are excluded. The same applies to social structures: those who do not function in the social play are excluded from the group, which severely diminishes their chances of survival in the animal kingdom.

Self-handicapping is one of those observed behaviours, also found in *hunter-gatherer cultures.* The foundation of play—which so naturally fosters both joy and learning in their way of life—undoubtedly lies in a deep-rooted culture of *autonomy and sharing.* There is much we can learn from this *(Gray 2011; 2015).*

As long as I am not willing *to let go of status or other hierarchical values* (such as "knowing best" or "being the most skilled"), playfulness will *not thrive.* Instead of genuine communication, there will be "talking to each other or over each other," and instead of true interaction, there will be "parallel play", much like when I was one year old.

To be in mutual communication means being in a dynamic, **balanced state of giving and receiving,** whether it involves an object, a situation, or another person.

For playfulness to expand, it is also about gaining self-awareness regarding Reciprocity.

I become aware of whether I tend to be more of a giver
or a receiver, more of a leader or a follower.

Once I understand this, I know what I need to be mindful of in life. By practicing my playfulness, I also become more balanced with regard to these poles. *I can be what is needed in a specific moment.* In this way, life becomes a place where I feel more at home—a place that is both mine and shared with others. I feel at home in whatever situation it may be.

- *Resonance*

The word resonance means "to sound back." Here, I refer to the spontaneous responses that arise within us in reaction to a specific action, event, or experience. By spontaneous, I mean that these responses are automatic and come from the more non-cognitive, non-rational areas of our soul—that is, not from logical reasoning or deliberation.

We humans are not walls that merely bounce back the ball thrown at us. When we are part of the game, we are allowed to be *whole individuals*, with all that we are. Unfortunately, this is often not the case. *School has largely shaped us to believe that only part of ourselves* counts. Perhaps this applies not only in school but throughout our waking hours—with friends, family, or in other contexts.

This is precisely what may stop playfulness in our lives. We are not used to including all parts of ourselves. In the midst of "play," something inside us may cause a string to vibrate, to resonate. And it is important that this inner tone is allowed to do so, that it is incorporated and included in the play and in life, for us to feel that the whole of us is valid.

Once again, this can be viewed from an artist's perspective. Here, it is not about the artistic drought, but about a terrible self-censorship. There is much that lives within, but on its way out, it encounters obstacles. What is needed here is to become aware of the inner resonance—the emotions or impulses that have been triggered—and then to include them in one's Interaction, in the playful engagement with life.

Impulsiveness

Impulsiveness is a value-laden word, often associated with recklessness, tactlessness, and disobedience. Impulsiveness often involves not having control over all the impulses that arise from within. An impulsive person does not struggle to follow their impulses; it happens naturally. What is needed to balance impulsiveness is compassion, attentiveness, and responsiveness.

In school, impulsiveness is often seen as "bad behavior." Over time, it doesn't work socially. But not enough time or space is given to channel this trait and allow it to mature through interaction with the world. This easily leads to impulsiveness becoming one-way communication, less receptive, and not developing social communication. It becomes a way of being but rarely leads to playfulness with others, despite its lively and perhaps creative outward appearance. What it needs is *time to mature*—which, of course, is quite obvious. Criticizing or punishing is of course counterproductive.

Research shows that impulsive children (such as those with ADHD) improve their social behavior when they are allowed to play freely, particularly through types of *Rough & Tumble-play* (wrestling games). This is believed to be due to the use and development of executive functions in the frontal lobe (Panksepp 2007).

Mutual resonance

Whether one feels full of impulses or feels numb inside (which is also not entirely uncommon), it is important to increase awareness of what and how it feels inside. We must include our inner feelings and impulses in life's play in order to make life more playful.

Naturally, human interaction also requires awareness of the other person's resonances. When playing with someone unaccustomed to listening inwardly, you may initially *need to do this for them* — to listen more deeply than surface-level engagement.

When interaction is resonant, the individuals involved form a whole greater than the sum of its parts — a dynamic, enduring space where creativity can thrive in a spirit of play.

Communicating with lifeless materials

But what happens when we interact not with another person, but with colours, musical instruments, clay, or other "inanimate" materials? How can something without a soul communicate resonance? Surely these objects have no inner life, no deeper layers. Yet, let us set aside this notion for a moment.

As a working model, we can choose to approach even "lifeless" material as though it were a living partner. To say that a colour "speaks" to me, that the characters in my novel reveal their innermost selves, or that a musical instrument "invites" me to play with it, not merely on it, might seem fanciful. Yet it is a powerful and effective method.

Interacting with what is in front of you — whether person or object — is essential for both play and creativity. When you listen closely and enter into genuine dialogue with a colour, a tone, a text, a stone, or anything else, creativity, playfulness, and what the psychologist *Mihaly Csikszentmihalyi calls Flow* are more likely to emerge.

Many artists — writers, painters, musicians, dancers — have spoken of how this dialogue with their material has unlocked a deep flow in their creative process. It can feel like playing catch with someone when the rhythm and communication between you and the "material" flow smoothly.

Perhaps this is simply a detour — *the material acting as a* **catalyst,** *awakening voices, emotions, and images hidden within ourselves.* Yet, I leave open the possibility that there may be more. Perhaps what we call dead matter holds its own kind of life, quietly conveying information to those who listen closely. I, for one, believe this could well be the case.

Interlude:
presence and interaction

"In the beginning was the presence."
Presence forms the foundation of interaction. Without a certain degree of mental presence, no genuine interaction can occur. A football team that performs poorly often does so because of a lack of interaction. Of course, other factors also play a role, but interaction is crucial — both in terms of pre-planned strategies and the unpredictable variables that lie beyond planning.

A deficient interaction can ultimately be traced back to a low level of mental presence. Even the most brilliant strategy in the world cannot compensate for this. The reality is that one can never fully predict what will happen on the pitch. On a detailed and subtle level, the unexpected will always occur — nuances that can have decisive significance. Only an alert and adaptable awareness — in other words, a good presence — can manage the challenges that arise along the way.

However, presence can be disrupted by many other factors — an aspect we will explore further later in the book.

In any case, without a significant degree of mental presence, there can be no real, playful, or genuine interaction.

The third element:

Dynamics

what is it?

For the greater part of my life, I have been engaged in the performing arts. I have taken part in hundreds of different productions and several thousands of performances or concerts. In these, I have been an actor, dancer, director, choreographer, musician, choir leader, and composer. A common thread running through all this stage and musical work has been the question of dynamics.

Even in my pedagogical work, a sense for the dynamic has been crucial to success—as it is in life in general.

The vitality and power of both life and art depend
on the dynamic way of handling it.

Dance, theatre, music as well as literature, poetry, visual art and even architecture draw strength from their dynamism. Film art moves between all these art forms and equally depends on **dynamics**.

*The word **dynamics** originates from the Greek dynamikos, meaning powerful, active, or possessing ability. It describes how a force operates in time and motion.*

One might say that dynamics describes how something ebbs and flows—like breathing, like the ocean's waves, like day and night, sleep and wakefulness. Whatever is dynamic is also **organic.** Organic, in the sense that what occurs rhythmically, as opposed to metrically (like a clock)—ever-changing.

Organic also in the sense that the dynamic shift in one direction never loses connection with where it came from — like a pendulum swinging to one side. Its path is determined by its origin, and it will inevitably return. It also adapts its tempo according to the circumstances — it slows before changing direction and accelerates into the new motion. In the case of a pendulum, this is, of course, governed by physical laws such as gravity and momentum. In the arts, as well as in social art and the creative playfulness that drives it, dynamics are shaped solely by our intuition, perception, and conscious choices. In Nature we can observe beautifully natural dynamics in cumulus clouds, ocean waves, and flowing water encountering obstacles. Even water trickling down an almost frictionless surface, such as a sheet of glass, exhibits dynamics. It does not take the most direct route down but instead meandering from side to side.

Dynamics is always an expression of an underlying force that creates shapes in time.

In my work with music and the performing arts — forms that exist within time — my focus on dynamics has grown continuously. As a composer, I do not perceive dynamics solely in terms of audible intensity (crescendo/diminuendo) but also within harmonic shifts and many other parameters.

When the **dynamics** are "right," a musical composition, theatre play, or choreography comes to life. "Right" means bringing to life what needs **dynamics**. When a theatrical piece for which I was responsible had lost its strength or presence, the issue was, of course, to revive it. This was achieved by *dynamizing* the piece — breathing life into it through dynamics rather than simply adding more material. Sometimes, it was a matter of simply removing elements to restore its natural flow — *akin to clearing debris from a stream that obstructs the water's movement (and interestingly, this is also the fundamental principle behind acupuncture and other holistic therapies).*

The same principles apply to playfulness and all forms of creativity.

Dynamics and playfulness

Dynamics is the vital force that bridges Presence and Interaction, **making them come alive and thrive together.** It is the ever-changing, active element that breathes life into both, allowing them to adapt and flourish in harmony. Without dynamics, presence becomes static, and interaction loses its vitality.

Dynamics is about recognizing the flow of the moment and responding accordingly. It involves shifting between states, adjusting rhythm and energy, and modulating the balance between polarities. This balance, however, is not fixed or centered — it is a dynamic equilibrium, one that evolves and adapts over time based on intuition and situational needs.

To engage with dynamics is to engage with life itself, finding the rhythm and energy that enable creativity, playfulness, and meaningful connection to emerge naturally. This is something I find immensely fascinating, as it touches on so many aspects of life.

Dynamics are about finding the "right breath," the "right rhythm," whether it concerns your own playfulness and creativity or the playfulness of the group or individuals you are guiding or teaching. The right dynamic — right for you or the group — is essential for sustaining playfulness. When playfulness endures, it creates an optimal situation, *one that reaches a higher level of creativity and a state of flow.*

A dynamic life relies on the ability to shift between the various qualities that make up dynamics. This ability develops as you attune to and follow the information that arises within you in relation to what you are engaging with — signalling when it is time to shift dynamically.

Let's take a very basic example, to illustrate what I mean. Your body has an innate ability — so long as it hasn't been disrupted or impaired — to adjust inhalation and exhalation according to its overall needs. This process is linked to muscle activity, oxygenation, the elimination of carbon dioxide, emotions, hormonal processes, and a range of other factors.

What the body does with breathing can be described as a *dynamic response to circumstances* — **a fundamental bodily dynamic.** As you're likely aware, breathing does not behave like clockwork, in-out, in-out. It doesn't have a metric quality. No, breathing has a rhythmical living dynamic — that's the least one can say.

Health and Dynamics

The same applies to sleeping, eating, and drinking. However, in reality, it is often the case that one or more of these rhythms, these dynamics, is disturbed. The Swedish National Public Health Survey (2024) reveals that nearly half (45 percent) of Swedes suffer from sleep problems. Various eating disorders are on the rise, and noticeable disruptions in breathing are also evident. This corruption of the body's natural self-regulating functions — a trend likely to continue — symptomatically reflects how we take care of ourselves and relate to others.

In light of the themes of this book, it's safe to say that many people lead fairly un-dynamic lives. Hectic, stressful, constantly rushing here and there, and at the same time far too sedentary. Living dynamically means striving for balance — a dynamic balance. Such a balance is never static but rather an ongoing process. The immune system and nervous system are constantly working to create this balance in the body. As conscious beings, we must actively and intentionally strive for it in our individual and social lives. It does not happen automatically.

Playfulness is a dynamic phenomenon. For it to continue within the activity you're engaged in, you must consciously respond to the signals your body and those you're interacting with send you.

Dynamic polarities

Presence and Interaction are like two siblings that thrive together. For them to flourish, they need Dynamics — the continuous modulation of their vitality. The "system" I'll share has proven most effective for me. It's rooted in my observations of play, creative processes, and social interactions. At its core are three pairs of polarities. I'll offer a fresh perspective on each, so for now, set aside any preconceived notions you might have. As we move forward, I'll explain how to practically manage these polarities

Dynamics consist of:

chaos—structure
stillness—wildness
on—off

To work with dynamics, I must always begin by acknowledging *how things are in the present moment* and then find my personal balance between these polarities. It's important to note that balance doesn't mean simply finding the middle ground between two opposites, like Chaos and Structure. The balance we're talking about is dynamic — a fluid equilibrium that evolves over time between the polarities. What I need to create in the moment, what I need to generate right now, might, for instance, be more chaos or more structure. *Only your intuition can guide you in making that decision.*

first polarity

chaos — structure

- *Chaos*

Extreme chaos is a state where nothing is yet manifested, but everything remains possible — potentially so. Healthy chaos is tied to consciousness and sensibility, but not cognition. Thought-based reflection, which relies on concepts, requires some form of structure to understand. Chaos, however, is the opposite of structure. Yet, there is consciousness within chaos. Its challenge lies in the absence of a comprehensible structure. Structure provides support and safety.

Consciousness, which demands a high level of attention, allows you to remain present in chaos. This attention, or sensibility, within Chaos, focuses not on specifics but on **the whole**—*on connections, relationships, the spaces in between, and the possibilities yet to be manifested.* Chaos is the mother of all things—*"Chaos is neighbour to God,"* as the saying goes.

When structure becomes too rigid, chaos must be introduced to restore balance. Only chaos can breathe life into something stagnant. This applies to everything — from political and societal situations to personal challenges. When something becomes stuck in structure, the spirit, vitality, and enthusiasm dissipate — just as they do when stuck in chaos. Both extremes, in their one-sidedness, lead to stagnation — culturally, psychologically, socially, and creatively.

Healthy chaos is conscious, sensible, exploratory, curious, and open to new possibilities. It requires a high level of awareness and sensitivity. In this state, you can discern the tendencies within the Chaos—what's ready to emerge. As a creator, you interpret these tendencies and act as a catalyst, allowing what best suits the moment to take form.

You cannot apply conventional thinking to Chaos. Doing so only reinforces what you already know — what feels safe. There is no progress in replacing one stagnant structure with another without first moving through a certain degree of chaos.

Think of it like breathing: you cannot inhale twice without exhaling in between. Chaos is the space where more than you ever anticipated becomes possible.

Of course, there is also unhealthy chaos — the destructive kind. This form of chaos stems from a lack of awareness of what is "moving within it." In such a state, you close your eyes and hope things will sort themselves out. Sometimes they do. But other times, chaos waits for your decision.

Remaining in this type of chaos for too long leads to a loss of breath — literally and figuratively. Everything loses its spirit and vitality.

Chaos has earned a bad reputation, which is understandable. Historically, it's been associated with disorder, war, and devastation. It's represented death and lawlessness. Nobody wants chaos, so we often over-organize, preferring the safety of the familiar over the uncertainty of the unknown. Chaos's connection to non-cognition stirs our fear of death — the unknown.

Confronting and embracing chaos, especially when something has become stuck in a structure, requires courage. It can feel like stepping onto a slackline without practice. But it may be necessary if it's what's needed to restore presence and interaction.

- *Structure*

At its extreme, the element of Structure dictates that only what is manifested holds importance. Anything not manifested is deemed insignificant. What can be measured, weighed, or defined in terms of time and space is what truly matters. The question is not whether something beyond what is currently visible and comprehensible exists, but rather where we direct our attention and what we consider meaningful. Our focus is drawn primarily to details rather than contexts and wholes — those are left to consciousness.

This might sound as though I favour chaos and dismiss structure, but that is not the case. Both polarities can be either constructive or destructive. When destructive, chaos leads to dissolution, whereas structure leads to stagnation — both culturally and mentally.

A healthy structure is tied to cognition, helping to organize and nourish the mind, but not directly to consciousness in the way I've described earlier. Structure brings order to our thinking, enabling reflection and reasoning. It represents organization — the framework within which ideas can form and develop. Every material possibility eventually manifests. The question is simply when, where, and how. What is manifested becomes tangible and challenges our creativity and playfulness.

An unhealthy structure, however, has exceeded its "expire date". If such a structure is sustained, life — like expired milk — turns sour. The not manifested, residing in Chaos, exists outside time, waiting for its moment, so to speak. *But once manifested, it is subject to time.* The most obvious example of this is a musical note. It is brought into existence by the musician, only to quickly vanish into the past as other notes await their turn to be played.

A structure might take the form of a rule for living, a social rule, or a rule of play — any kind of rule. In theatre, it might appear as a prop, choreography, or another kind of spatial or temporal framework. Structure could be the limitations of a material, the constraints of a fellow player, or even your own boundaries. In short, it encompasses anything that is, in some way, manifested.

Structure always originates from something that was once a possibility — something that may have been appropriate to manifest in the past, whether a second ago, a minute, a day, or a year. But everything has its time, and the time for rebalancing often comes sooner rather than later.

In practice

Do I need more of Chaos?

Could it be that the activity I have chosen to engage in lacks openness to what has not yet been manifested? Has my focus become fixated on what I already know, what I am already capable of, and what has already been materialized? Do I feel paralyzed by these limitations?

Perhaps I need to challenge myself more or allow for a greater element of chaos? I could do this by embracing uncertainty, stepping into a state of not-knowing, and thereby heightening my awareness and attention. Maybe I need to shift my focus away from the details and instead attune myself more to the bigger picture — to connections, contexts, and the spaces in between, in the broadest sense? Perhaps I need to listen more intensely to the context and the wholeness in order to discover what wants to emerge?

...or do I need more of structure? Could it be that the activity I have chosen to engage in lacks meaningful structure, such as clear rules to follow, or a focus on the limitations (properties) of the materials or individuals I am interacting with? Is there a lack of direction or framework in what I am doing? Am I losing myself in the paradise of possibilities and therefore need to structure my actions, challenge my mind? Do my actions require more structure to guide me back onto the path of creative playfulness?

Interlude: Trees or Forest

Consciousness — which, more than cognition, aligns with the Chaos element — has more in common with **hearing** than with seeing. Hearing, in its broadest sense, can learn to move from its innate and natural holistic experience of hearing to focus on the particular — like the distant song of a bird.
That is like starting to perceive the trees within the forest.

It is, in essence, *seeing what you hear.*

Cognition, however — which, more than consciousness, aligns with the Structure element — has more in common with **seeing** than with hearing. What seeing does, as an innate ability, is observe, register, and reflect. It stimulates the analytical part of us, dividing the world into fragments and categories. What seeing should learn is to zoom out a bit and thus begin to perceive the bigger picture.
That is like starting to perceive the forest that holds the trees.

It is, in essence, *hearing what you see.*

"Start perceiving the forest that holds the trees" emphasizes shifting focus from the individual details (the trees) to the broader context (the forest). It encourages a more expansive view that acknowledges how all elements interact within a larger system.

Instead of concentrating solely on isolated parts, this approach asks you to recognize the environment or framework that holds them. It's about perceiving connections, relationships, and patterns, and understanding that the whole ecosystem — like the forest — is made up of *interdependent* components that work together. This shift helps you perceive not only what is immediately visible but also the underlying structures that hold everything together.

"Start perceiving the trees within the forest" shifts the focus back to the individual elements — the trees — within the larger system, the forest. It suggests that while understanding the broader picture (the forest) is essential, paying attention to the details (the trees) is equally important.

This perspective encourages you to appreciate both the whole and the parts. It's about recognizing the unique qualities and characteristics of each tree, yet understanding that each tree is part of a larger, interconnected whole. This way, you can see how individual elements contribute to and interact within a bigger structure, and how every detail, no matter how small, has its place and significance within the greater context.

To see what you hear and hear what you see is like breathing.
Light and air comes in through the perception.When you truly listen with your eyes and look with your ears, you are attuned to the full spectrum of sensory input. You do not merely observe or hear separately; you allow them to blend, creating a fuller, more nuanced experience. This way of perceiving goes beyond the obvious, where the boundaries between different senses blur, and your awareness expands to include both the concrete and the abstract.

---

second polarity

wildness — stillness

- *Wildness*

Wildness is about approaching the unknown. It is about testing the boundaries of my abilities, whether they relate to the body, the social or the mind. It's a playful exploration of limits, to see what is possible, to discover what experiences lie ahead.

In interactions, the emphasis lies on *doing*. It is through a deep dedication to the act of doing. It is through *surrendering myself to the activity*, that I can be surprised — surprised by myself, surprised by others, surprised by the material in my hands and surprised by what happens between me and the person or situation I am engaging with.

- *Stillness*

In contrast to Wildness, the polarity of Stillness pertains to staying within boundaries. Here, there is no play with limits; instead, we remain within what is familiar, what feels safe — the 'comfort zone.' In interactions, the focus is on being. Even in playful or creative activities, and despite their intensity, the emphasis is not on the act of doing itself, but on simply being in the moment, present and engaged.

In practice

You notice that your presence or the quality of your interaction is declining. Could it be that the interaction is too demanding and challenging? Am I retreating, partially shutting down, to avoid being overwhelmed by information?

Perhaps I should slow things down and seek something more familiar — without losing the playfulness or the creative process. In fact, by rediscovering my rhythm and aligning the challenges to match where I am in the moment, I can find myself entering a new flow state, one marked by a heightened sense of presence and connection.

Or...

you notice that your presence or the quality of your interaction is declining. Could it be that I am becoming too comfortable, almost drowsy? The safety feels too great; I recognise too many elements. It has all become too familiar. The activity isn't challenging enough, and I am losing interest. Perhaps I should introduce some challenges, test my own or our collective abilities? Maybe by increasing the pace? Perhaps by altering the conditions — figuratively speaking, venturing further out on the branch?

third polarity

on — off

- *On*

"On" primarily refers to the decision to enter into presence and interaction. It may also involve expanding or sharpening focus on what has been chosen to engage with. Intensifying or increasing the pace is also associated with the "On" polarity. It can also involve an elevated level of cognition, memory, concentration, perception, or innovation.

- Off

"Off" primarily concerns concluding the activity, and deciding to step away from the task. It may also involve reducing the scope of focus or loosening the sharpness of concentration. Slowing down or reducing the intensity of action is also associated with the "Off" polarity. It can also involve lowering the level of cognition, memory, concentration, or perception. Letting go, forgetting, or leaving things behind naturally belong to the "Off" element.

Intensity

A key factor in managing the dynamics of on and off is intensity. Nothing is ever purely on or off—there are countless shades in between. Imagine a scale from 1 to 10, where 10 is maximum intensity (100% on) and 1 is complete absence of it (100% off).

The level of intensity is linked to the energy you invest and how focused or directed that energy is. For instance, in a social situation where anticipation builds before something happens, very little energy is spent on action, yet the intensity is high because most of the energy is held back, sharpening presence and attention.

Alternatively, two people may engage in an intense dance, with fast tempo and complex movements. Despite the physical effort, their mental state is relaxed, and all their energy is purely focused on the movements—this is where the intensity lies.

Intensity can also be tied to tempo but is not the same. For example, you could drive at 120 km/h with low intensity, settled into a long motorway journey, or at 30 km/h with high intensity, frustrated by a slow car ahead. Both scenarios show that intensity is about focus, engagement, and presence, not just speed.

In practice

I notice that my presence or interaction is diminishing in quality and strength. What can I do dynamically? Does this indicate that it's time to increase the pace, or do I need to intensify? Or is the opposite required: should I slow down the pace and intensity? Is it time to increase or loosen concentration? Is it memory or forgetfulness that is obstructing playfulness? Is it perhaps time for me to take a break from the doing, letting go of everything for a moment or for now... or is it time to make a new decision to continue?

The creative process: The On and Off

*Especially when exploring the **creative process,** one can observe a kind of **organic ebb and flow** (off and on)—an underlying rhythm that operates beyond talent and dedicated craftsmanship. One might call it a "creative breath"— a rhythmic alternation between exhalation, pause, and inhalation, much like natural, functional breathing.*

This creative process unfolds in three distinct phases.
*In the **first phase**, the artist or scientist fully immerses themselves in their subject of inquiry. They engage deeply with the material, driven by willpower, intensity, and focused effort.*

*The **second phase** requires a complete release of focus— whether through sleep or by shifting attention elsewhere. During this stage, the material explored in the first phase is processed, internalized, and transformed, integrating with deeper impulses, information, and knowledge.*

*When the time is right, the **third phase** begins, allowing the processed material to surface as new insights, creative solutions, and fresh ideas.*

*In **The Courage to Create,** Rollo May examines these stages in greater depth, offering historical examples to illustrate their significance.*

Intuition

Intuition

So how can you know when to change the dynamics?
How do you know when to shift towards Chaos or Structure,
Wildness or Stillness? How do you know when it is time to
Start or End, to slow down or speed up, or to change the
intensity?

The primary factor is having gained knowledge and
understanding of what these polarities can entail. It is like
adding more strings to your lyre. The crucial question revolves
around timing and execution, meaning: When should I shift,
how, and to what degree?

Picture this: You've decided to be fully present in a given
activity, aware of what you're focusing on, and maintaining a
relatively undisturbed presence. You're engaging, ensuring that
you sustain contact with the object of your interaction — there's
mutuality, listening, communication, and inner resonance. Yet,
despite all this, the interaction and your presence will eventually
falter if you fail to handle these elements dynamically. It is the
dynamics that keep them alive. What is needed, then, is
Intuition.

Playing Jazz

When I use the word intuition, I am referring to something
highly pragmatic. Let me describe how it manifests for a
musician. Intuition is hardly a word commonly used in musical

circles. Instead, they refer to musicality. The way I use these terms, there is no difference. A skilled musician is intuitive in their playing. To be musical is to be intuitive in musical expression.

Imagine an improvising jazz band. Timing, rhythm, intonation, and direct communication between musicians are put to the ultimate test. The parameters of When, What, and How become even more critical since there is neither sheet music nor a conductor for guidance. It is a wonder that it usually works. The precise moment when and how a note is placed involves such subtleties that the thinking brain has no chance of keeping up.

However, it is through intuition that the musician, in the moment, without conscious thought or reflection, finds the answer to When and How. Or rather: The answer directly manifests in execution without an intermediary thinking process. The musician simply knows—through an inner, somatic knowing.

In a state of musical flow, the musician remains aware of what is happening, yet the performance unfolds independently of conscious thought. In fact, entering this flow requires letting go of rational, logical thinking. The body instinctively knows What, When, and How—often before the mind has even caught up.

There must be "feeling" when making music — emotional listening and allowance for feeling. But it is not feeling or emotion that plays "the right note at the right time." *Emotion is like a wave the musician can surf on.* The emotional wave is necessary; it carries and provides energy for the performance.

But it is intuition—deeply embedded in the body—that knows how to navigate the surfboard, moving in sync with the other surfers in the band.

How often have I witnessed musicality—meaning intuition —deepen, expand, or flourish when a group's listening shifts from just the ears to the entire body? When **the whole body** listens and engages in musical interaction, intuition awakens. The intelligence of the body **is** the intelligence of intuition, and in a musical context, this is what we call being truly musical (and it doesn't have to be jazz).

The Intuitive Dance

Let us observe a dancing couple in a dance with elements of improvisation, such as Argentine Tango or "Contact Improvisation." Everything flows. Intentions and movement impulses flash between the two bodies at lightning speed. They are completely in sync. Both possess a well-developed spatial and kinaesthetic awareness, but it is as if they think with the same brain. They are attentive and aware of what is happening, but it is not the cognitive centers of the brain that are primarily active — not conscious decision-making. All co-movement and all sensory information exchanged between the dancers must happen simultaneously. Only then does a shared flow emerge.

Information that enters through the senses must return with a response. To prevent the processing of this information from disrupting the shared flow, thinking must be *delegated to the body*. However, this is a different kind of consciousness than the one used for daily reflection, recollection, or cognitive processing. Nor is it akin to dream-like consciousness, which involves an inner observation of images.

Intuitive consciousness is about waking up in actions and events before they happen.

In this way, the follower in the dance knows "in their body" what is about to happen a fraction of a second before it occurs. And in this way, the musician knows which note, rhythm, or key change is "on its way," despite being fully absorbed in the present moment.

Intuition as a Compass

*Intuition is a bodily awareness that provides direct impulses and information about **how, what, and when.** By direct, I mean impulses that are immediately **compatible** with action. For instance, shifting from a structured state into one with a small degree of chaos, subtly altering intensity or tempo, or the unmistakable signal that NOW is the time to conclude and step away.*

Intuition can handle everything from necessary split-second decisions that save lives to subtle shifts that allow playfulness to continue evolving into new realms.

In our modern era, intuitive consciousness has been overshadowed by cognitive reasoning. Rationality takes precedence over emotion. Control takes precedence over intuition. Our habitual desire to foresee the future and our compulsive need for guarantees that things will go well deafen us to the inner impulses and information — intuitions — that could position us and our actions correctly in the game of life, in playfulness, and in creativity.

Developing intuition

However, intuition is something that can be developed and nurtured. *It grows as you begin to listen to subtle signals and trust them.* You must listen, and you must trust them. The more you listen and the more you trust them, the clearer and more audible they become. It is that simple — and that difficult. Because it requires courage. Trust is about courage. Trust is about daring to relinquish control over the future.

You can either choose to try to control the future — which you will never succeed in — or you can choose presence and trust. But I promise you that the latter will make your life more playful and creative. And it will also be a life that aligns far better with who you are and what you truly desire. That is the only guarantee that can be given.

Intuition and Conscience

Intuition as a state of consciousness is closely related to what is called *conscience.* I do not mean good or bad conscience, but simply conscience. The word conscience consists of two parts: "con" (together) and "science" (knowing). This is the case in many languages. In some languages, like German, conscience is *Gewissen* which literally means "inner knowing".

Conscience — *to know together and simultaneously.* This gives a clue to what conscience fundamentally entails. Conscience is not about **conventional** notions of right or wrong. At its core, it is about sensing whether an action was erroneous or just. Whether it was right or wrong depends less on convention and more on the specific moment and context in which the action was performed.

To "know together"; to have a conscience, is to be in contact with *the collective consciousness.* It is the same field in which intuition operates. One could call this the "In-Between Field," the "Intuition Field." Quantum physics refers to it as the "Quantum Field" or the "Field of Possibilities," pointing to a reality that has *not yet been physically manifested,* but which "**contains all information about everything**" — in contrast to the "field of the manifested," the sensory reality we can weigh and measure.

> *The definition of what is impure or even evil depends on when and where it occurs. The value, meaning, and consequence of a specific action are **not** absolute but are determined by the spatial and temporal context—and intention. All awareness of right and wrong under these circumstances is called **moral intuition.***

Resonance in action

To "know from the periphery," from the collective consciousness, might seem to oppose knowing from "deep within." Yet, this overlooks the fact that we, ourselves, every single individual, are part of the collective. In my interaction with the world around me, what I know "most deeply" will, in truth, be that which resonates with my surroundings.

A *resonance in action* — a form of interaction that is in harmony with the world (like a single instrument within an orchestra) — arises when my innermost being is attuned to the external world. Freedom lies in whether I choose to follow this resonance or not.

As Viktor Frankl reminds us, the ultimate freedom is to choose a response or attitude "that works" — for both myself and the world around me.

The difference between blindly following one's impulses (impulsivity) and acting intuitively is consciousness. Intuition is one of the forms of consciousness available to us — and one we can cultivate. Outwardly, the two may appear the same. Yet inwardly, there is a presence of mind, an awareness that sees and notes what is happening, and how these intuitive impulses manifest.

Intuition always provides a direct, actionable response to:

What?

When?

How?

Dynamics: Summary

Playfulness, like creativity, is sustained by interaction and presence. For these to endure and thrive, they must be managed dynamically. Dynamics flow fluidly between various polarities: structure and chaos, wildness and stillness, on and off (intensity).

To understand, in the very moment, how to handle a situation dynamically, you need intuition. Intuition is an awareness in action that provides bodily perceptible signals and impulses for action. These signals inform you about what, how, and when a dynamic shift needs to occur. The signals are always directly compatible with and transferable into action. The more you listen inwardly and trust the internal information you receive, the more accessible the intuitive information becomes.

Repetition: The core elements
*...of what is needed to create
playfulness or elevate creativity?*

Presence

Choice of Focus

Inner Silence

*You need to know what you want to focus on,
and the quieter your inner state, the more information
you will perceive from what you focus on.*

*This creates a sense of time and space dissolving,
where the only important thing is what you focus on.*

Interaction

Connection

Reciprocity

Resonance

You need to maintain contact with the person or thing you are interacting with and ensure a balanced lead-and-follow.
Additionally, you must allow the deeper, inner aspects of both yourself and your counterpart unrestricted access to the interaction — without losing connection or reciprocity.

This creates a sense of flow and connection within the interaction and an almost inexhaustible source of energy.

Dynamics

Wildness—Stillness

Chaos—Structure

On—Off
(Intensity-level)

Using your intuitive ability, you need to discern when, what, and how to shift from one dynamic element to another, to what extent, and at what pace, in order to maintain high-quality Presence and Interaction.

This creates a sense of rhythmic, dynamically breathing life.

repetition of core elements

Interlude:
Mihaly Csikszentmihaly and the concept of Flow

In this book, I frequently use the term "flow." It is a widely recognised concept today, and most people have some understanding of what it means. We have all observed the movement of water in a stream—how it flows smoothly around and over obstacles, how it swirls, bubbles, and moves forward, always following its course through the landscape. The obstacles are merely something it dances around.

Flow is an excellent word to describe, for instance, a creative or social situation that works, has dynamism, and develops naturally. The term is likely as old as humanity itself, but in modern times it has become a concept within psychology.
What psychologists describe as the "flow state" is remarkably close to what one might call the "playful state."
*Both are based on similar fundamental conditions. One could also say that what Csikszentmihalyi describes as the "**flow state**" is what one achieves through what I describe as playfulness.*

"Flow" is a central concept in psychology, developed by Mihaly Csikszentmihalyi in 1975 after years of research on creativity, play, and the personalities of artists. His interest stemmed from a desire to understand what makes certain activities so motivating and engaging for individuals. At that time, enjoyment and positive experiences were relatively unexplored within psychology, which was dominated by behaviorism's focus on reward and punishment.

In his book *Beyond Boredom and Anxiety* (1975), Csikszentmihalyi introduced the term "flow" to describe the state in which a person becomes fully immersed in an activity, losing track of time and self-awareness while simultaneously experiencing deep control and satisfaction. He observed this state in artists, musicians, athletes, and others engaged in complex and absorbing tasks.

Csikszentmihalyi argued that flow provides a key to understanding motivation and human well-being. He challenged the prevailing view that work and learning must be dutiful and unpleasant. Instead, he proposed that activities that generate enjoyment and flow could contribute to personal growth and the cultural evolution of society.

Components and Characteristics

Csikszentmihalyi identified several key factors that characterise the *flow* state:

- **Merging of activity and awareness**: The individual feels at one with the task and acts effortlessly without overthinking.

- **Loss of self-consciousness**: Thoughts about the self and the external world become irrelevant, with the individual entirely focused on the present moment.

- **Sense of control**: The person feels an inner strength and confidence in managing the task and its demands.

- **Clear focus and feedback**: Goals and strategies are explicit, and feedback from the task is immediate and comprehensible.

- **Autotelic nature**: The activity is inherently rewarding and does not rely on external incentives.

According to Csikszentmihalyi, flow is both an enjoyable and functional experience that motivates people to seek challenges and raise their standards to re-experience this state.

Flow in Psychological and Biological Perspectives

Csikszentmihalyi linked *flow* to brain function, particularly the prefrontal cortex, whose activity decreases during *flow* — a phenomenon known as hypofrontality. This reduction silences irrelevant thoughts, allowing the individual to concentrate on the task without mental fatigue. The dopamine system is also activated during *flow*, explaining why the state feels so rewarding and motivating.

In summary, Mihaly Csikszentmihalyi's research on flow has profoundly influenced how we understand motivation, performance, and quality of life. By exploring what makes activities meaningful and enjoyable, he opened the door to new approaches for creating more engaging and enriching life experiences.

PART 2

Practicing
Playfulness

How to practice playfulness and creativity

Here I will present a collection of exercises designed to develop your ability to be present, to interact, and foster dynamics—individually or in a group.

You may recognize some of the exercises described below, but it is essential to note the unique context in which they are placed here. Every exercise has a purpose, and this purpose, or intention, is crucial. It influences how you perform the exercise and the results you achieve. *The intention acts as a catalyst that gives the exercise its direction and depth.* That is why it is important to remind yourself of your personal intention with a specific exercise — in other words, what you wish to achieve through the practice, and what it is you hope to develop.

In this context, the exercises are about supporting and developing playfulness and creativity. They are designed to strengthen specific aspects of playfulness and should be performed with a conscious intention: to improve your ability to interact, be present, or cultivate dynamics. By keeping this intention during your practice, you will be able to deepen your understanding and develop these abilities richly and purposefully.

The Role of the Senses in Presence and Awareness

Presence and focus in a healthy body depend largely on the function of the senses. The senses can be likened to windows that connect the external world with our perceiving consciousness. It is through these "windows" that sensory impressions keep awareness alert, helping us become fully present in the here and now.

> *Experiments in the 1960s by John C. Lilly on sensory deprivation in "sensory isolation tanks" demonstrated the negative effects of **eliminating** external sensory stimuli on consciousness, cognitive ability, and decisiveness—leading to disorientation, anxiety, and hallucinations. These research findings laid the foundation for the development of various training programmes for astronauts.*

However, the generation of clear awareness through the senses occurs only partially—sensory experience can be *deepened and expanded through increased inner activity.* When we are motivated, interested, focused, or engaged, our sensory awareness intensifies. Interest and motivation are closely linked to free will. When our focus and engagement stem from a *self-motivated decision,* we perceive more of what the senses communicate, making our experience of the world richer and more nuanced.

Voluntary engagement and personal involvement activate the brain's dopamine system, which is strongly connected to the system of reward and motivation. Motivation also influences activity in the prefrontal cortex—the part of the brain responsible for decision-making—providing us with greater *endurance* in maintaining presence.

A heightened state of awareness can, of course, also be triggered by imminent danger. This type of presence activates numerous neurological and metabolic functions in the body, preparing it for "fight or flight." However, what distinguishes this acute presence from the voluntary, self-motivated kind is that it does not lead to stress and tension. Instead, inner stillness can be combined with increased perception—something long recognised in the practice of *martial arts.* I often refer to this as being **"restfully awake"** or **"wakefully resting."**

The exercises described here are designed to *sharpen the senses and heighten awareness without being tied to stress or fear.* Instead, they aim to consciously awaken the sensory organs and allow them to deepen the connection with the outside world in a relaxed and open manner. In doing so, we not only train our senses but also our ability to be present and attentive.

The opening of the senses

Practicing presence and engaging with the sensory world also serves as a way to "awaken the senses," metaphorically opening the sensory windows. The more you engage with these presence/sensory exercises, the deeper and clearer your sensory experiences become, and the more information can reach your consciousness. As the sensory world reveals itself more fully, it also becomes a source of inspiration, joy, and renewal.

The sensory organs are, figuratively speaking, like delicate flower buds. Treated correctly, they open up. If subjected to mistreatment, they close up again. In modern civilisation, we are overwhelmed by a flood of sensory impressions. The sensory system must adapt to noise, chaos, smog, and synthetics in all their forms, *resulting in dulled perception.* The senses become increasingly deaf, blind, and numb. Alternatively, an imbalance may occur when certain sensory organs overwhelm the system with excessive information, exceeding the capacity for processing. This can result in stress, which over time may develop into *chronic stress and hypersensitivity issues.*

Be prepared for the fact that the presence exercises I describe here **will** increasingly open your senses. Over time, you will become a sensory connoisseur. You will grow more sensitive, but you will not become hypersensitive. Since these exercises are intended to enhance your presence, they will simultaneously *strengthen your stable inner core.*
Figuratively speaking: if you raise your "sensory sails," you must also increase the weight of your stabilising keel. The mental and physical grounding that keeps you upright is as necessary as the heavy or deep keel on a sailboat raising large sails, preventing it from capsizing.

So, while you practise presence, your sensory organs will, as a side effect, open, and your experiences in the sensory world will grow deeper, more colourful, and filled with richer tones, fragrances, tastes, and forms. Eventually your synaesthetic abilities will develop. Synesthesia is a neurological phenomenon where sensory impressions merge, such as hearing colours or seeing sounds.
If you are a creator of dance, theatre, music, or visual art, an endless sea of inspiring "material" from the sensory realm will open itself to you.

Exercises for presence

- *Touch*

The sense of touch allows us to experience boundaries.
When your body comes into contact with something, you become aware of where the boundary of your body is in relation to what you touch. Through touch, you encounter something other than yourself and receive numerous and varied impressions and information.

Exercise 1: exploring contact

Lie in a resting position—on your side, back, or stomach, stretched out or curled up. Occasionally, but not too often, change your position and then hold it for a while. Begin by exploring which parts of your body are in contact with the floor. Direct your presence to these contact areas and experience the size of the area, the amount of pressure, or the weight transferred through the contact point.
Once you feel ready, move your attention to the "bridges" formed between one contact point and another. Note the difference between the bridges and the contact points (bridge supports). Feel how the muscles, ligaments, and skeleton contribute to these sensations.
The experience of the muscles forming bridges is also a tactile sensation. The interaction of muscles with other muscles, ligaments, and the skeletal structure, as well as the pressure and tension in the joints — all of these are internal sensations and perceptions of boundaries and surfaces.

Exercise 2: inner presence

Sit or lie comfortably, remaining still. Imagine an "inner body" filling your physical body, a system of energy that gives it life and form. Direct your awareness to this inner body and experience its subtle sensations. Whether you perceive it as energy or simply blood flow is irrelevant; what matters is focusing on something so subtle that it demands increasing concentration and inner stillness from you. This hones your ability to be present.

Exercise 3: conscious touch

Let your hands consciously touch your own skin as if it belonged to someone else. Become aware of your body's boundaries. Explore the shapes of your body parts, the textures, the temperature etc

Exercise 4: conscious touch of other objects — and bodies

A) Extend this conscious touch to the objects around you—a table, a cup, the ground, a tree, or even a pet—as if you were encountering them for the very first time. Awaken the curious child within you. Close your eyes to heighten your sense of touch. Notice the temperature, texture, softness or hardness, resistance, and shape. Let your hands and fingers trace the object's contours, sensing the concave and convex, the sharp and the smooth. Explore touch beyond your fingertips—use the backs of your hands, your cheek, your arm, or even your back to discover new tactile sensations.

B) If possible, incorporate these exercises into touching a living person. The challenge of maintaining presence in the act of touch itself now becomes greater. Any recognition or thought that it is a person—someone you know—must be set aside by **deepening your sensory awareness** and staying fully present in the experience of touch.

Be mindful that you are not trying to understand anything about the object. Instead, the focus is on practicing presence through sensory experience. For understanding or recognition, you must create an inner distance necessary for reflection and comprehension. When that happens, presence diminishes. Presence is wordless and thoughtless. It is being itself, in perception and action.

Make conscious, present touch a part of your daily life. Each time you take a moment to engage in touch mindfully and non-reflectively, even if only for 15 seconds, you receive the present moment as it is. This can give the experience of time standing still for a while (which is also characteristic of the play- or flow-state). You invest a little time in presence and gain tenfold in return.

Through this practice, your "presence muscle" will grow. It will benefit you in your interactions with others. Without presence, there is no engagement, no playfulness, and no creative flow.

- *Movement*

The sense organ referred to here is the one that perceives movement. Whether I see, feel, or otherwise experience movement, the body's muscles and nervous system correspond to the perceived motion. What I experience of movement thus comes from my own body — even when I am entirely passive and observing someone else's movement. Even when I merely think about or dream of movements, the nervous and muscular systems are activated.

It is a distinct form of perception and could just as well be referred to as the sense of self-movement.

Exercise 1: free breathing

Lie on your back. Relax your jaw and let your mouth remain open, allowing air to flow freely through both your mouth and nose. Let your body alone manage the breathing. Close your eyes and be an alert observer of how your body breathes. Notice how the air flows out and in, how the abdomen rises and falls. Above all, observe the pause in breathing your body takes after each exhalation. Let it last as long as the body wants. Allow the body itself to give the impulse for the next inhalation. Witness how the breathing occurs. Notice how this *movement of your breathing body* feels.

Exercise 2: structured breathing

Sit upright. Breathe through your nose. Choose a specific breathing structure, for example, 4/2/4/2 — that is, about 4 seconds for inhalation, 2 seconds for holding, 4 seconds for exhalation, and 2 seconds for holding. Gradually slow down the breathing and counting with each cycle. Another structure is 4/8/4, that is, about 4 seconds for inhalation, 8 for exhalation, and 4 for holding. The advantage of the latter structure is that it activates the parasympathetic nervous system, which contributes to relaxation and rest.

You practice presence in motion by simply being present in this simple breathing rhythm. Notice every small detail of the breathing and how the body responds to this breathing structure.

You can practice this regularly every day, but you can also do it whenever you want or need. It may be enough to close your eyes and be present for three simple, slow breaths.

Exercise 3: conscious walking:

This presence exercise is best done barefoot, but if shoes are necessary, that works too.

Step 1: Slow down your walking to a pace where you feel you can be fully at *one with the act of walking.* You could call it *"your personal tempo at this moment."* Walk with awareness of your walking and your body as a whole.

Step 2: After a while, gradually decrease your pace further toward zero, but never to zero. Now, increase your awareness of the movement in your legs, feet, and toes, as well as the motion of the joints and muscles. Sink your presence into the movement. *The slower you move, the more your ability to be present is challenged and exercised.* However, it is also true that the slower you move, the more detailed information you gather about the movement itself and its components.

Choose to bring your awareness to **a)** either a specific group of muscles, such as the ankle joint or **b)** the connection between different joints such as the knee joint and the ankle joint, or **c)** the relationship between one leg and the other. Be clear with yourself about which of the two focus areas you choose: individual details or connections (coordination).

Exercise 4: Free Movement:

Let your body move freely—no set structure, no planning. Simply allow the body to lead the way. Let the movement be slow so that your consciousness has time to experience everything happening in your joints and muscles. Notice how your experience changes—for example, when your arm is extended versus bent or when a muscle is tensed versus relaxed. Observe the relationship of one body part to another, whether in motion or stillness. The list of what you can discover could go on endlessly. But it is certainly not about seeking plenty. You are practicing presence, and here the old saying in the performing arts applies: *"Less is more!"* What is "more" is the presence itself, and it is difficult to create a presence around too many details, novelties, and innovations. You are not trying to create a new dance. You are simply aiming to be present in the little that you do.

4b: Just as with walking, slow the exercise down more and more, eventually to the edge of stillness — but not actually stillness. And just as with walking, you choose to bring your awareness to either a part of the body, such as the movement of the hand itself, and, or the connections, such as the movement of the hand in relation to the body (distance, direction, etc.).

4c: Finally, practice distributing your presence across the whole body and its movement as a totality. You are practicing holding the entire movement of your body in your awareness — as a unified whole.

4d: The next step is to use your bodily total-presence to keep the entire body in simultaneous motion — no part of the body may ever be still. You will understand that you need to be extremely slow to accomplish this final part with complete bodily presence.

Be clear with yourself about which of the different stages (4a-d) of the exercise you choose.

Exercise 5: Structured Movement

Perhaps you engage in dance, Tai Chi, or another movement discipline. Take a specific element from your movement library and, with the help of presence, work your way into the smallest details. Discover aspects and qualities you were previously unaware of because you had not devoted the same level of presence to these elements before. However, your aim now is not to discover something new. Your aim is to enhance your capacity for presence. The discoveries will be gifts along the way.

Exercise 6: Perceiving the Movements Around You

These presence exercises focus on experiencing the movements in your surroundings as perceived through your vision, while you yourself remain still. Remember that the experience of movement always takes place within your own body, even when observing movement in someone or something else. With that in mind, stay open to sensations within yourself as you witness movement around you.

Be still in both body and mind, and immerse yourself in the experience of someone else's movement, or a movement taking place in nature — clouds, flowing water, and so on. Be present in their movement. Let your perception melt into it. Your observation should be free from reflection, conclusions, and judgement. Experience as intensely as you can through your senses. The intensity of this exercise can escalate to the point where you ultimately feel the other person's movement within your own muscular system.

6b: The same exercise, but now with your eyes closed. Stay close to whatever is moving and remain present with the sensations of movement you now perceive in a different way. The experience of movement may be conveyed through hearing, a sense of warmth, or another sense.

- Hearing

Let your presence fade into the world of sounds around you!

Close your eyes and immerse yourself in the sounds with your presence. Set aside reflection and recognition, and simply experience. Imagine that you can enter the *inside of every sound* you hear, and thereby, so to speak, get inside the sound itself or the source producing it. "From the perspective of **sensory opening**, your ability to sink into the sounds and their sources will grow stronger with practice.

Notice the difference between categorically distinct sources of sound.

Exercise 1: Nature Sounds
Explore and fade into sounds of wind in leaves, babbling water, droplets, the resonance of stones, various kinds of wood and metals, fire, explosions, engines, etc. There is no end to the number of natural (or mechanical) sounds one can find. But it's not about the quantity of sounds; it's about how present you can be with each individual sound, how deeply you can listen in to the material you've chosen.

Exercise 2: Vocal Sounds

Explore and fade into sounds from something that carries consciousness. Sounds from various animals and the voices and sounds of humans.

Animals: When you listen to animals, keep reflection and recognition away. Also, keep at bay any feelings or emotions that might arise within you, as these draw you away from the object into the subjective — your personal associations, references, and previous experiences. You do this by enhancing your presence. The exercise is to remain in the sensory experience of the object. Hear the sounds as sounds themselves, not as communicative sound signals (even though they usually are).

Humans: The same applies to human voices. When listening to human voices, you can also practice "listening beyond" the singing voice or the words spoken. Singing evokes musical emotions. Words engage the intellect. In this exercise, you are to keep both intellect and emotion away, focusing solely on perception and experience.

There is no limit to how deeply you can listen into a being as long as you "listen beyond" your intellect, avoiding conclusions and judgements. Listening to speech and voice without hearing the words or making judgments about the voice itself is a challenging and highly presence-demanding exercise. Inner stillness and silence are tested.

- *Music*

As a phenomenon, music moves between two worlds, two sides of reality.

- **The tones, sounds, and timbres**—those vibrational frequencies you perceive with your sense of hearing, transmitted through the air, water, or any other medium.

- **The spaces in between** — that which does **not** sound, that are not physical vibrations. The intentional pauses or silences between one tonal or sound expression and the next. These in-between spaces can be filled with sound or be silent, but in musical terms, the space, the interval, the pause, serve as a bridge or pathway from one point to the next, from one note or sound or other element to the next. This movement from one "point" to the next and then the next is the essence of music. Music is an internal motion that creates an emotional movement within the listener. It is from this internal listening that the musician creates music with audible tones, sounds or other elements.
The sounds create a sensory experience comparable to experiencing colour or fragrance. However, the music itself is not a sensory experience but an entirely immaterial experience within one's own soul. It is, therefore, not audible.

The musical presence exercise involves:

1.   To distinguish between the audible and the inaudible in the overall musical experience. What is inaudible yet an essential part of music and the musical flow?

2.   Deepening your presence and experience in the sounds and tones of the instruments or voices — the audible aspect. Try to perceive the audible aspect of the music as if you were seeing and touching substances, textures, and colours.

3.   Distinguishing between the tone itself and the sound colour, the "timbre", that is given the tone. For example, the tone A from a clarinet and a flute differ in sound colour (timbre). The clarinet has a darker, woody, and richer sound with many overtones, while the flute produces a lighter, purer, and more transparent tone.

4.   Deepening your presence and experience in the tone as such. How do you experience the tone? Can you perceive it in your own body, in a specific place?

5.   Deepening your presence in the musical experience — that what is *inaudible* and only internally perceivable. Examine within yourself the experiences of, for example, movements, colors, or emotions that arise. Immerse yourself in these sensations.

6.   Differentiate in your perception (non-intellectually) between melody, harmony, beat and rhythm, and deepen your presence in each of them, one at a time.
When you, for example, immerse yourself in melody, do not let the rhythm influence the experience, and vice versa.

In this way, not only does your hearing open up to the

individual elements, revealing their secrets, but your presence also grows.

A further deepening of presence can be undertaken in the realm of music. This offers an endless playground for a true sound enthusiast to refine their capacity for presence.

Music

- Seeing

The presence exercise consists of distinguishing categorically different elements in what you can see with the physical eye.

Distinguish between:

- *Shapes and colours*

- *Lines and surfaces*

- *Light and darkness*

Choose the area in which you wish to deepen your presence.

For example, you are standing in a landscape with a forest on the other side of a field. You find all the above categories present and now you make a choice.

Exercise 1:

You choose to deepen your presence in the forest's colour nuances. You eliminate lines and shapes from your perception as much as possible and allow yourself to be absorbed solely by the colours. You fade into the green color—the various shades of green. You allow the green to fill your entire experience, letting yourself become one with the green; you become green; you explore the world of green.

Exercise 2:

You focus on the lines—the curves and straights—that define the forest's silhouette, letting your awareness follow their flow until nothing else matters. Notice how time is embedded in the perception of a line, just as it is with shapes—unlike surfaces and colors.

By choosing a single element and immersing yourself in its perception—whether the overall shape of the forest or the shifting interplay of light and shadow —you refine your ability to focus. The essence of this presence exercise lies in isolating one category of perception while filtering out the rest.

Through practice, your capacity for presence deepens. In this way, you strengthen your awareness and can even develop your own presence exercises. You'll begin to recognize what challenges your focus. But now you also know that by refining it, presence becomes both a powerful foundation for creativity and playfulness—expanding your ability to interact—and an ever-opening channel for information and inspiration.

"Gazing in couples"

"Gazing" is a beautifully subtle presence exercise that engages multiple senses. Seeing is definitely not the only one of them. One could almost speak of, when it works at its best, a sense that thoughtlessly and wordlessly experiences the partners "self"–a "self-sense".

Sit in pairs, facing each other, and rest your gaze in the other's eyes—nothing else happens. The goal is to remain completely still within, simply allowing the gaze to rest. You are both a receiver and a giver, yet you do not hold onto any thoughts, emotions, or sensations that arise. Instead, you stay in a state of wakeful stillness, fully present in the gaze. Agree on the duration of the exercise beforehand and set a timer.

Method for Sense Exercises

One approach to structuring these exercises is that they can be arranged in an entirely different order than the one I have set out.

Regarding presence exercises in *movement,* it may be better to start from the other end, that is, with free movement (Exercise 4), but in a wild and unconscious way, as if to dance out the excess, and then gradually introduce awareness into the movements — slowing down the pace, narrowing the focus of presence, and moving towards conscious walking (Exercise 3), followed by Exercise 2 and then Exercise 1. After that, Exercise 6 (movements outside yourself) should be practiced. Always return to Exercise 6. This trains the perception of the finest muscular movements within your own body, those that imitate in an almost imperceptible way.

When it comes to *listening* to sound or seeing what you see, a good method is to alternate between focusing on a limited area and taking in the whole. For example, switch between focusing on rhythm or timbre and experiencing the ocean of sound or the music as a whole.

In terms of *sight*, alternate between immersing yourself in colours or lines and "listening" to the overall impression of the landscape.

Both in deepening your perception of the individual element and in absorbing the whole, the aim is to grasp as much as possible with your presence. When listening to the whole in the visible or audible, it is about spreading your presence across the entire "field" of impressions. When you do this, you become aware not only of individual elements (and simultaneously) but also of the connections and the spaces in between. If this is applied within the field of vision, you develop a "special skill" in your presence that I call "listening through the eyes." If you do this within the field of listening, you develop a "special skill" that I call musical.

- Pain and Presence

Pain or Suffering

A common obstacle to playfulness and creativity is physical or emotional suffering. How often have I witnessed how a person's emotional suffering has prevented them from fully engaging in interaction—an interaction that could have been healing for them? It is therefore important to explore how to change your relationship with pain, so that it does not lead to suffering, which lowers your presence and hinders your creativity.

Pain can be understood as an intense, localized, involuntary presence caused by a factor beyond our control. It arises when we injure ourselves, feel sorrow, or suffer from an illness. The body or soul then sends signals, calling for our attention. Suffering, however, is something different—it is the attempt to distance oneself from pain. One does not want to feel it, so one turns away. Yet pain does not disappear simply because we resist it. Instead, it becomes a battle we are bound to lose. Suffering consumes our presence, drawing it into the experience of itself.

But unlike pain, **suffering** is a choice. That may sound harsh, especially to someone enduring immense hardship. Viktor Frankl, a survivor of three years in concentration camps under Hitler and later the founder of logotherapy, wrote: *"Everything can be taken from a man but one thing—the last of the human freedoms: to choose one's attitude in any given set of circumstances."*

Our greatest freedom is the ability to choose how we relate to what is and how it is. Frankl argued that meaning is not something passively received but something we create. And with meaning, we find the motivation to endure, to act, and to live. It does not erase pain, but it is the way out of suffering.

The dual purpose of practicing presence with pain

When it comes to pain, the result of practicing presence is twofold. Firstly, it strongly **enhances your overall ability to be present.** Secondly, the effect of practicing presence in pain is that **you will suffer less from the pain** — whether it is physical or emotional. In turn, **this reduces the pain itself** and creates more space to possibly understand the root causes of a specific pain. And in turn it gives more space to engage in creativity with life.

Perspective and approach

Something crucial in our relationship with pain is how we think about it. If we think or even say the words, *"I am sad"* or *"I am afraid!"* we are asserting that *I am what I experience.* We identify with the pain. The *I* is the subject that experiences, and the *experience* is the object. By thinking or saying *"I am sad"*, we reinforce the idea that the subject and the object are one and the same. This is not an issue when the object represents something positive and uplifting, such as *"I am happy!"* But when the object (such as fear) is something that could lead to

suffering the result is not desirable. It lowers our creativity and
our ability to interact with life. Moreover, the more intense the
object — be it body pain or grief — the more the subject and
object are drawn together and "want" to become one. In that
state, you are, so to speak, locked inside your pain.

Pre-Exercise 1: emotional pain

When in emotional pain, try thinking *"I experience sorrow"* or *"I
experience fear!"* If you adopt this way of thinking and shift your
perspective on pain, you create a separation between object and
subject — between sorrow and yourself. This does **not** mean you
experience less sorrow, but it gives you the option *to choose to be
present* in it. It is precisely this small space of freedom that arises
between *You* and *Sorrow*, between subject and object, that allows you
to focus your presence on sorrow, rather than be consumed by it. As
you already know: creativity is conditioned by free will and the free
decision to be present.

Such an inner space of freedom also provides strength — the
strength needed to remain present. Fear and anxiety will take on a
completely different meaning for you. There is a distinction between
experiencing fear and *being afraid* of fear itself. The latter tends to
generate anxiety. An important insight is that anxiety in general, and
panic attacks in particular, often stem from a *fear of fear* — an anxiety
about anxiety itself.

Thus, practice saying:
"I experience fear."
"I experience anxiety."
"I experience sorrow."

The consequence of this new approach is that fear or sorrow
simply becomes another experience among many — just like joy,
anger, and other emotions.

Pre-Exercise 2: physical pain

Here, too, a different perspective can make a difference and increase your capacity for presence.

If you have back pain, instead of saying 'I have back pain,' say: " I am *experiencing* pain in my back"

This separates the object (pain) from the subject (you) and creates that small but crucial inner space of freedom needed to remain present with the pain. Again: you may not be able to remove the pain, but you choose to experience it. This choice has a decisive impact on how you continue to perceive the pain.

> *People I have met who have endured great emotional and/or physical pain — and who have chosen to go through it, to experience it fully — have demonstrated a remarkable capacity for presence and the inner peace that comes with it.*

Pre-Exercise 3: upgrading the new perspective

A refinement of this approach to emotional and/or physical pain is to reframe it in the following way:

"I am in a room of sorrow."
"I am in a room of fear."
"I am in a room of experienced pain in my back."

By phrasing it this way—both in thought and speech—you reinforce that you are the one experiencing the pain, rather than being defined by it. A room has walls and doors—you can enter and exit. Now, imagine feeling trapped in an endless space of pain or sorrow. For some, that is their reality. This is why the thought *"I am in a room of..."* is so powerful—it gives you the ultimate freedom to relate to your pain on your terms. And you can *choose* presence.

Summary

Experiencing physical or emotional pain often leads to suffering. When you suffer, your level of presence decreases, and as a result, interaction, playfulness, and creativity deteriorate. By eliminating suffering, only the experience of pain remains. That pain should not be eliminated — you can choose to step into it with your full presence. The best way to do this is by shifting your perspective on pain, recognizing it as just one experience among many. This leads to two outcomes: first, the pain itself feels less overwhelming, and second, your overall capacity for presence grows.

Exercise 1: Breathing

Bring your awareness to your breath. Allow it to slow down gradually. Let your exhalation be longer than your inhalation. You can extend your exhalation by providing slight resistance with your teeth and lips (as in the sound "Fffff"), or even more effectively, by humming a tone with your mouth closed using the sound "NG" (as in the word *lung*). This will activate the vagus nerve, which in turn stimulates the parasympathetic nervous system, helping you to become calmer and making it easier for you to remain present with whatever arises.

Maintain this type of breathing, humming, or toning throughout the following exercise.

- For Physical pain

If your pain is physical, direct your presence to the specific area where you feel it. Let your awareness gently sink into the pain site.

Let your awareness move toward the very epicentre of the pain. Fill yourself with **curiosity** about that place.

Stage 1: At times, it may be difficult to locate the precise epicentre of a pain, but let that remain your intention and working model. The accuracy of its physiological location is not the primary concern. What matters is the method itself — the model of presence. Imagine yourself as an explorer venturing into a cave, courageously navigating toward the core of your bodily pain.

Stage 2: Once you reach the epicentre, generate a sense of peace — regardless of how it feels — and *plant* that peace within the area. Set the intention to rest there for a while, quietly observing the space. What can you see? What can you feel? What is happening there? These questions are **not** meant to elicit answers. Their sole purpose is to encourage presence.

Throughout this exercise, keep all judgments and conclusions at bay. Your role is not to analyse or interpret but simply to *be there* and *experience*. Be firm with yourself in this regard.

If, for any reason, the pain suddenly intensifies, summon the courage to go even deeper into the epicentre. Resist the impulse to withdraw. What can be helpful here is to **hum,** *combined with an increased local presence. (The humming, like singing, is always a manifestation of will— in this case, an affirming will. And, as mentioned, it also increases relaxation and calm in the body).*

Stage 3: After a time, leave the space while generating a sense of lightness. Imagine yourself rising up and returning to reality like an air bubble ascending through the water in a lake.

- For Emotional pain

If your pain is emotional, continue the breathing, humming, or toning as described earlier, *maintaining this practice throughout the entire exercise.*

Stage 1: locate the emotional pain within your body — as if it had a physical epicentre. The precise location you choose does not need to have any psychosomatic validity. The working model itself is what matters. This approach facilitates your ability to be present. By situating emotional pain in the body, you bring it closer to the *now*, since both the body and breath exist in the present moment, whereas emotions stem from the past. Anchoring emotions in the body allows you to experience them purely, free from thoughts and interpretations.

Rather than triggering thoughts, conclusions, or associations — which lead to *absence* — allow your emotional pain to be *an experience*, *as tangible as physical pain.*

Stage 2: Once you have identified (or chosen) the bodily epicentre of your emotion, *generate a feeling of peace* — regardless of how it feels — and *plant* that peace within the space. Set the intention to *rest there* for a while as you explore what it is like. **What can you see? What can you feel? What is happening there?** These questions do not seek answers; they exist solely to cultivate presence.

Stage 3: When you feel complete with stage 2, allow your emotion, along with the feeling of stillness, to expand and flow in all directions—down into your legs, arms, and beyond your body. Then, release the exercise.

The Healing Power of Presence

To the extent that I am able to be present — and of course, this is dependent on the magnitude of the pain — I will notice that the pain diminishes, perhaps even disappears, or at the very least remains as a bodily sensation but without suffering. This is the effect of *the strength of presence*. This is the healing power of being fully present.

If, on the other hand, I carry a hidden agenda throughout the process — the aim of *eliminating* the pain — then I am working against myself. The task you give yourself, freely and willingly, is simply to be present.

This exercises is to be used whenever needed. It remains, at its core, a practice of presence. Yet, it has a remarkable secondary effect: it transforms the very experience of pain.

Finally, life presents us with pain, but we retain our ultimate freedom to relate to it however we choose. We all wish to engage in playfulness and creativity — qualities that make life meaningful because they illuminate and *bring forth* life itself. And *life*, when fully lived, holds an inherent sense of meaning. That is simply how it is. The task is to live it.

Yet, life's pain can obstruct our desire to fully live. This is when you make the conscious decision to regard pain as an *offering*, an opportunity to practise presence at a high level — and to emerge from it with gold in your hands and an ever-deepening capacity for presence.

Summary on pain:

- *Pain and suffering are two distinct phenomena.*

- *Suffering depletes the presence you need for interaction.*

- *By intentionally increasing your presence in the pain and moving towards its epicentre, you eliminate suffering.*

- *Presence creates a sense of wholeness and is, therefore, healing and alleviates pain.*

- *The presence-strength you develop by practicing presence in pain becomes available to you in all interactions, growing into an ever-stronger capacity.*

- *Pain does not have to hinder interaction as long as you include it in your presence and engagement.*

- *The opportunity of manifesting the "ultimate freedom".*

"Everything can be taken from a man but one thing:
the last of the human freedoms —
to choose one's attitude
in any given set of circumstances,
to choose one's own way."

         Viktor E. Frankl

how to practice   presence   method

Exercises for Interaction

Practicing Interaction

You practice interaction best with others.

In fact, the whole of life can be a training ground. At the same time, you cannot go through life with a constant ambition to practice. What, then, happens to spontaneity, to the fresh breeze of life? You must primarily live and experience life. And in doing so, you may come to realize that if only my interaction with life were a little deeper, even more life would emerge from it! Your desire may not directly concern interaction itself but rather something beyond it — perhaps the wish for your relationships to function better, whether at work or at home, with adults or with children. It could be that you long for greater creativity in a certain area or the ability to experience life more intensely and playfully. And one of the keys, as I have said, is Interaction.

Practicing interaction

The interaction exercises, such as the ones I describe below, is a unique opportunity to step into something together with others for a limited time. During that moment, you are permitted to leave everyday life outside, which allows you to invest more energy and attention in what you and your companions are about to do.

An interaction exercise also makes certain essential elements of interaction more apparent and and provides an opportunity to target specific areas that require more attention than others. In everyday life, the ability **to be both a good giver and a good**

receiver (Reciprocity) is mixed with personal relationships, stress, prestige, ambition, social anxiety, and so on. But during these exercises or games, the moment can be free from most of those influences. This allows for a more concentrated practice and development of the fundamental aspects that enable good interaction in life — while also being enjoyable, *as it should be*.

Fascilitating

As a pedagogue, when I work with a group of children or adults, I observe what is lacking in the interaction and then design or modify an exercise or game to specifically develop that missing element. *Naturally, presence as attention is always practised in every interaction exercise.*

You can also increase your awareness of what **you** may be lacking in interaction — what is undermining it or making it feel unfulfilling. When something is playful, it always feels meaningful to continue.
Is it your approach that hinders playfulness?
Is there something missing in the reciprocity — perhaps in your ability to give or let go, or in your ability to receive or respond?" You can explore these questions further using the **troubleshooting chapter.**

Later on, I will provide examples of group interaction exercises. Some of these are purely movement-based, while others are traditional games that can be used as training platforms.

Practise on your own

However, if you do not currently have access to a partner or a group with whom to practise interactive movement, you can always begin with the interaction that should already exist within your own body — namely, the motor coordination between its different parts.

Example: Toss an object, such as a ball, from one hand to the other. Once this no longer feels demanding, introduce an additional object, then another, and another — you are now juggling. There is no limit to how complex this internal bodily interaction can become. At the same time, you are laying a physical body foundation that strengthens your ability to

interact with others. When you juggle, your body parts must continuously adapt to ever-changing circumstances. Your body must both initiate the play and remain flexible in response to the momentary relationship between the involved body parts, as well as external forces such as gravity, momentum, and energy.

Another example in the same category is balancing — whether by walking along a narrow surface such as a plank or a slackline or by balancing objects in different ways. Climbing trees or rocks, practicing parkour, learning new dance steps, or engaging in similar activities also fall into this group.

What those examples have in common is that they challenge your presence in an activity requiring *coordination.* They all develop your flexibility—*your ability to adjust to the circumstances of the present moment.* It is also about the body's interaction with itself, and through that, establishing a solid, self-affirming, and bodily experiential foundation for interaction with others.

Mastering any of the above *does not* automatically make you a skilled interactive participant with others — many other factors must align, as discussed in previous chapters. However, you are building a bodily foundation for presence, flexibility, and balance. What you establish in the body often becomes more accessible in psychosocial interactions. This has been repeatedly confirmed in various settings, such as conversations, collaborations, and other forms of interaction, where participants first engaged in interactive movement exercises. Many have reported noticeable improvements in their ability to connect and cooperate. **This is why there is a growing interest in interventions of this kind, such as inviting a workshop leader to work with leadership teams, corporate groups, or school classes.** These interventions primarily consist of movement exercises and games that, in an indirect yet catalytic manner, resolve issues related to teamwork and communication.

The practice without ambition
and the playfulness within the practice.

*Important! For an exercise or game to be truly effective and yield the best results, it is essential that it is **not** performed for the sake of improvement. It must be carried out for its own intrinsic value. The beneficial and desirable consequences of the practice should remain by-products. This principle is closely tied to a fundamental aspect of play: play is done for its own sake. If a participant is focused on an external goal — such as developing a specific skill — then their attention is diverted to something beyond the present moment. This diminishes their presence, which in turn weakens their ability to interact effectively.*

*This is the paradox of play: it fosters development, but only on the condition that one does not focus on what they hope to develop. The same applies to training. To achieve the best results, an element of play must always be present. The rule is clear: **never practise without an essential degree of playfulness.***

The following exercises primarily train interaction, but at the same time, they also develop presence and attentiveness. Some of these exercises, through their demanding sensitivity, help to refine the perceptual faculty for dynamics.

I am presenting only a selection of the exercises I have practised over approximately 35 years — specifically, those to which I have most frequently returned. These are the exercises where I have observed the best results.

And by a good result, I mean that the exercise has influenced the rest of life in terms of interaction and communication in various forms. The exercise has not remained an isolated skill confined to the practice space but has fulfilled its purpose in enriching playful, creative, and social life. The exercises have, of course, been modified, and some have been excluded depending on the age of the participants (ranging from 6 to 75 years old). It is up to your observations and judgment to determine how and what you choose to implement.

Always base your decisions on direct observation, not preconceived ideas.

It is impossible for me to describe these exercises in a way that allows you to understand them exactly as I intend and have personally performed them. However, let that not be an obstacle. Instead, let these descriptions spark your imagination regarding how a particular exercise should be carried out. Observe it in action, clarify for yourself the intention behind it. — The intention is essential to any form of practice, for it provides direction. — So, let these descriptions inspire you to create exercises based on the needs you perceive.

Group Movement Exercises

These exercises focus on the group as a whole. Participants should cultivate a "soft focus," meaning they never fixate on any single person or object but instead maintain a wide, panoramic awareness, absorbing information from the entire group.

”Mingling"

The group moves with a constant, even flow, covering the entire space and weaving around each other. Physical contact is avoided. The participants should maintain a steady and healthy flow in their movement through the room. Work at an elevated pace to challenge your attention.

Mission 1: Move around each other as much as possible with high intensity.

Mission 2: Constantly seek out empty spaces and fill them with your movement (variations in tempo allowed).

- Upgrade: "Mingling with Push and Pull”

Participants can briefly exert a soft, light and short push or pull on others as they pass. The affected individual must *always respond fluidly and flexibly,* without resistance, letting the touch affect the movement in space. The focus remains on maintaining a smooth flow.

”Hunter—Hunted"

Similar to the previous exercise, but now incorporating the imaginative shift between feeling like a *hunter* or being *hunted*. The movement is more dynamic and expressive, fluctuating between near-stillness and rapid motion. Participants may explore different positions — crouching, moving upright, or even moving on all fours.

”Forward—Backward"

The group moves intensively in a fast-paced, mingling fashion with arms extended forward to more easily navigate around others.

On a signal from the leader (e.g., a clap), everyone stops, closes their eyes, and begins moving backwards in slow motion. Another signal returns the group to rapid forward movement. The transitions between these states become increasingly frequent. Physical contact should be avoided, but any accidental touches should be handled smoothly and instinctively.

”Object Exchange”

The group mingles at a steady, continuous pace, smoothly **passing on** objects they hold in their hands. It is beneficial to use objects of varying sizes. In a group of, for example, 15 people, there are around 7 objects, more or less. The emphasis is on the flow of movement and the smoothness of giving and receiving. To begin with, physical contact is avoided.

- **Variation 1:** The group is then instructed to **expand** within the space and subsequently **contract** until physical contact becomes unavoidable due to crowding. However, this should not disrupt the flow and fluidity of movement. Expand, contract, expand and so on.

- **Variation2:** With eyes closed.

Variation 3: With eyes closed and moving backwards.

Note: In variations 2 and 3 the tempo is reduced, but smoothness and flow must be maintained.

...with Synchronised Change

”Stop—Start”

The group moves fluidly in a mingling fashion. At any moment, *anyone* can decide to initiate a full **stop,** which the entire group must immediately follow. The only way to signal this stop is by halting one's own movement — no verbal or external cues are allowed.

Restarting occurs the same way: one person resumes movement, and the entire group must follow suit in perfect synchrony. The goal is to reach such a level of attunement that an observer *cannot tell* who initiated the stop or the start.

The challenge for the group is to discover how to achieve this level of synchronisation. The challenge for each individual is how to subtly lead without being obvious, and how to perceive and respond to the shifts initiated by others. Who initiates the change is always the result of a spontaneous impulse from someone in the group.

    - **Upgrade:** The exercise remains as above but with the addition of new elements. To the options of Start and Stop, further actions are now introduced, one after another. Here is a small list of suggestions:

— **Start**
— **Stop**
— **Jerk suddenly**
— **Rotate half a turn**
— **Go down on all fours**
— **Move on all fours**
— **Stand up and say "Ooooooh Hey!"**
— **Gradually change speed between slow motion and running**

Add one element at a time. Either establish a set sequence for the agreed-upon actions or let them occur randomly.

”Bird Formation”

This exercise is inspired by the way large flocks of birds move synchronously in clusters. It focuses on improvisational and synchronized group movement, where *leadership* is passed from one person to another.

The group is evenly spread out across the entire room, all facing the same direction. At the front of the group, one person improvises movement. They do so in a simple way and slow enough for the entire group to remain fully synchronized and precise in their following. The leader moves continuously in a frontal direction. When the leader turns to either side, the front of the group automatically shifts, and the leadership transitions to the person who is now in the new front position.

It can either be left completely open as to who becomes the leader of the flock, or it can be predetermined which, for example, four individuals (positioned in each of the cardinal directions) will take turns leading.

- **Variation:** The above exercise can also be performed with three people standing in a triangular formation or with two people, one positioned behind the other. This opens up possibilities for variations where leadership changes occur rapidly or where faster and more extreme movements are allowed. In this case, it becomes impossible to synchronize the movements exactly, but instead, the focus shifts to moving in the same manner rather than in perfect unison.

...with Touch

"Push and Guide"

Pairs work together using the principles of push and guide. It is not permitted to block, hook, or hold onto the other person. *Both participants act as leaders and followers simultaneously, co-creating the movement together.*

Version 1: Partners remain in contact only with their hands, pushing and guiding each other while adapting their stance and body positioning accordingly. *Both participants act as leaders and followers simultaneously,* co-creating the movement together.

Version 2: As above, but now including forearms in addition to hands. This can be further upgraded to involve the upper arms and shoulders.

Both versions can be performed with different levels of pressure:

1.   **Feather-light contact**, using minimal muscle engagement.

2.   **More intense pressure**, where greater muscle strength is involved.

"Push or Pull, Follow or Resist"

This exercise builds upon *Push and Guide*, where participants explore the four elements: push, pull, follow, and resist. They let their bodies act and react—using push or pulling, following the other's movement initiative, or momentarily blocking the motion.

However, any blockage or resisting should last no more than a few seconds–to not break the flow but change it.

Variant 1: One participant leads, using only push or pull, while the other responds by either following or blocking:

Variant 2: Both participants take on the roles of leader and follower simultaneously, intuitively co-creating the movement using push, pull, follow, and stop.

- in both variants, play with the options of applying either **feather-light contact** or **more intense pressure.**

"Rolling Point"

This is a paired exercise based on constant bodily pressure. Any part of the body can serve as the contact point. The objective is to move while allowing the contact point to shift across the body surface, without sliding. Imagine balancing a small ball between you and your partner, rolling it across each other's bodies without letting it drop or jump between points. Symmetry is not necessary.

Upgrade: Use a physical ball, such as a tennis ball or squash ball, to refine the movement.

"Pair Flow with Bridges"

Pairs face each other, holding hands. Multiple pairs move fluidly throughout the room. Every time they approach another pair, they must decide instantly whether to form a bridge for the other pair to pass under or to pass under a bridge formed by the other pair. The movement should be light, fast, and seamless.

"Trio Flow"

Three people hold hands throughout the exercise (though they may need to adjust their grip as the movement unfolds). The goal is *continuous* and very slow movement, where all participants constantly shift their positioning relative to one another. The movement should remain fluid and organic, with no one acting as the sole leader — each participant must simultaneously initiate and follow. The bodies should remain in constant motion, regardless of the position they find themselves in.

"The Group Knot"

Participants stand in a circle and take each other's hands, holding on until the exercise is complete. Together, they work to create a group knot, making it as intricate as possible. Once the knot is fully formed, everyone closes their eyes and begins to untangle it—without letting go—until the group has returned to a circle.

”Triangles”

Everybody moves freely around the space. Each participant secretly selects two other people. (These individuals may, of course, have chosen their own two different secret people — this remains unknown to everyone.) Throughout the exercise, you relate to your chosen two as if forming a triangle. By continuously moving, you strive to create an *equilateral triangle* with them, which proves to be quite challenging, as they are simultaneously adjusting *their* positions in relation to others, attempting to form their own equilateral triangles. This results in a constant, chaotic, yet sensitive movement throughout the space. You adjust your pace as needed. You avoid colliding with others.

- **Upgrade:** Occasionally, an equilateral triangle may briefly emerge. The moment this happens, you immediately run through your own triangle to the other side, aiming to establish the same triangle from a different perspective.

”Give and Receive Weight”

This exercise is performed in **pairs.**

Person **A** stands upright and remains still. Person **B** moves around A, selects a place on A's torso or upper arms, and places both hands on that chosen area (one hand on top of the other). **A** then leans into this support. **B** yields gradually, allowing A to transfer more and more of his / her weight onto B's hands, to the extent that **B** permits the angle of the lean.

Important! Person B should not increase the lean (and thus the weight transfer) beyond what they can support, and they must be able to guide A back to the original upright position. B, in turn, should ensure they have a stable and balanced stance before transferring their weight. Once B has returned A to their original position, they release contact, B circle around A, and repeat the process from another angle.

Initially, A should place their hands only on the upper part of the trunk. In an **advanced** version, A may use other parts of the body as contact points, such as the hip, knee, or head.

Significant Upgrade: **A** takes control of deciding in which direction to lean and which part of the body requires support from **B** — *without using verbal communication.*
B must remain highly attentive to perceive **A**'s decision and move swiftly to provide support, preventing **A** from falling to the ground.

Variation: You may choose either the basic form or the upgraded version, but the **roles** of supporter and weight-giver *should continuously alternate.* One moment, you give weight; the next, you provide support. The goal is to create a *seamless flow in these transitions* — so that it "feels like a dance."

"*Trio Throw*"
This exercise involves three participants: A, B, and C.

1. **A** stands still and throws an object (such as a soft ball) straight up into the air.

2. **B** runs towards **A** and moves them away (essentially "rescuing"**A**).

3. **C** rushes to the spot where **A** was standing, catches the falling object, and then moves to a new position.

4. Now, **C** becomes the thrower, **A** becomes the rescuer, and **B** becomes the catcher.

5. In the third round, B throws, C rescues B, and A catches. The cycle then continues in this manner without breaks, maintaining a continuous flow.

The exercise should run for many rounds without interruption in movement. When performed smoothly, the tempo increases, demanding a high level of attention and coordination among all participants.

(In the original version, a genuine brick was used instead of a ball, which made participants extraordinarily attentive.)

...with Clapping

"Flow Clap"

Everyone stands in a circle. A clap is passed around the circle with emphasis on maintaining a steady, even flow.

Upgrades:

Introduce multiple ongoing claps, where a new clap starts before the previous one completes its round.

Allow free changes in direction.

Variation 1: Multiple claps moving simultaneously in both directions.

Variation 2: Increase the speed while maintaining the flow.

"Move into the Room"

The same as "Flow Clap," but instead of standing in a circle, the group moves freely around the room, passing one or more claps in an unstructured manner.

"Rhythm Circle"

Similar to "Flow Clap," but performed in a three-beat rhythm, meaning *every third clap* should be emphasized.

Upgrades:
- Replace every third clap with a stomp.
- Experiment with other time signatures, e.g., 3+4+3+4 etc meaning every third and fourth clap is replaced with a stomp, creating a seven-beat rhythm.

If the flow is disrupted due to rhythmic complexity, simplify accordingly. This exercise can be advanced indefinitely by incorporating different time signatures, body parts, circular movements, and pair-based rhythms.

"Give & Receive Clap"

The group stands in a circle. Each participant receives a clap with a clap and passes it on with a second clap, ensuring smoothness and evenness in rhythm.

Variation 1: As above, but with the addition that anyone, at any time, and as many people as desired, can run to the other side. Act on impulse. When this happens, a gap appears behind you, and a crowd forms where you arrive. However, everyone in the circle works to create even spacing between all by adjusting their position. (Note: You do not take the gift with you when you run).

Variation 2: Move freely in the room while passing the clap at random (every participant has one receive clap and one clap pass it on).

Variation 3: The recipient's receiving clap should be simultaneous with the giver's giving clap.

Upgrade: Participants must keep their eyes on the clap at all times without disrupting their movement flow.

”Chaos Clap"

Participants stand in a circle (ideally no larger than 12 people). A clap is passed across the circle to anyone except the two adjacent people. The aim is to keep the tempo as high as possible — imagine a pinball bouncing rapidly within a machine.

”The Wild Clap Upgrade"

In this version of the clapping exercise, quick Flow Claps are passed around the circle, including direction changes, and are combined with cross-circle claps (”Chaos clap”).

You can also add vocalised syllables: **"Hoo"** when passing the clap along the circle, **"Ha!"** when changing direction, and **"Hey!"** when sending the clap across the circle. It should be fast-paced, but the flow must be maintained throughout.

...with Sticks (or balls)

The sticks I've used the most, and which work really well, are bamboo sticks, approximately 60 cm long and about 2 cm thick. Larger and heavier sticks have also been used. Tennis balls or juggling balls are a good – and in many ways softer – alternative.

"Chaos Stick in a Circle"

Everyone stands in a circle, using one (1) throwing stick. The stick must only be thrown across the circle, never to the two closest neighbours. Unlike "Chaos Clap," the focus here is not speed but smoothness. The throw and reception of the stick should be rhythmical, soft, and fluid. Any jerkiness should be eliminated, with an emphasis on gentleness.

Upgrades:

1. Introduce a second stick, which is passed around the circle rather than thrown.

2. Add a third stick, which, like the first, is thrown randomly across the circle, but independently of the other thrown stick. Now, three sticks are in play, requiring a high level of focus and attention.

3. Continue adding sticks as long as the group can handle them. Also add sticks that are not to be thrown but instead *passed from hand to hand.*

Variation 1: Dissolve the circle and **move freely around the room**. Make sure to use the entire space. Keep throwing one or more sticks to each other. Remind them to keep their movements free and to use the entire space. The goal is to dissolve the conflict between throwing/receiving the sticks and moving freely

Variation 1B: like above but now *Add* a few additional objects that are not to be thrown but instead *passed from hand to hand.*

Upgrade: If the exercise is conducted in a room lit solely by electric light, gradually reduce the lighting, making the space progressively darker.

Three Resonance Exercises

As you may recall, interaction is based on *Contact, Reciprocity, and Resonance.* The interaction exercises above emphasize Contact and Reciprocity, as well as Presence. You will notice how these elements develop through the degree of *Flow* the exercises achieve. The increasingly strong presence and the ever-smoother flow that arises are indicators of good interaction. However, *Resonance* is not particularly emphasized in these exercises. Yet resonance is crucial for participation to integrate the deeper aspects of one's creativity and playful interaction. ***It enhances the sense of coherence.*** This sense of belonging is fundamental for long-term engagement to feel meaningful.

Often, when a recurring creative practice has lost its sense of meaning (in other words, has lost its playfulness), it may be because one has not fully *integrated oneself* into what one is doing. One is not fully present with one's whole being. The following three exercises focus on the *internal process* that takes place before one responds. Initially, the flow must be sacrificed. It is essential to ensure that the *input* is received deeply, that it resonates internally, and that the *output* emerges from that *resonance.* As a result, the dialogue must progress slowly and deliberately.

This type of fundamental exercise can be found in theater schools, where, since the early 1900s, the concept of Authenticity has been central. In a dramatic dialogue, responses should not bounce back and forth like a ball between two walls (comedy is different). Instead, the ball should enter the actor, resonate, and only then be returned once something deep inside has been touched. The response must be **authentic.**

”Yes—No”

In pairs, stand facing each other. You take turns speaking. You may only say one word at a time, and the only words you have at your disposal are Yes! or No!

For example, Person A might say, Yes! Now it is Person B's turn to say Yes or No. There are a thousand different ways to say Yes or No, and that is the essence of the exercise. It is not about inventing a way to say Yes or No, but about truly receiving the Yes or No from your partner — *letting it sink in, feeling how it affects you, and allowing your own Yes or No, your response, to be shaped and coloured by that experience.*

Always search the response true to you–true in that very moment.

You will notice just how much can actually be expressed using only one of these two words.

  Note: you may only say *one* word at a time. The dialogue continues in this manner, with both partners allowing the other's word to enter their soul, strike a chord, and then return in the form of one of the two words.

Avoid falling into a comedic **routine** *or following a pre-planned pattern. Allow yourself to be surprised — both by yourself and by your partner — and follow the flow, no matter where it leads.*

”Gesture Dialogue”

This exercise follows the same structure as the one above, but instead of words, you use gestures. The number of possible gestures is unlimited, but you may only make *one* gesture at a time.

Observe your partner's gesture and let it sink in. A single gesture can carry an immense range of meanings — for the one performing it and for the one receiving it. What matters, however, is the *internal experience* it creates within you. That inner response is what should shape and influence the gesture you give in return as a response.

Always search the response true to you–true in that very moment.

”Movement Dialogue”
This exercise follows the same structure as the previous two, with one key difference: the "words" you use are neither concrete words nor concrete gestures but ***abstract movements.***

Words and gestures always represent something concrete — something that can be thought about and put into words. An abstract movement, however — such as an arm motion, a tilt of the head, or a step — can be performed without expression, as a neutral movement. The same movements can, of course, also be carried out with intention and expression. However, in this exercise, the movements should remain **expressionless** and be performed in a neutral manner.

Yet, despite this neutrality, it is inevitable that your partner, witnessing your movement, will form an impression of it. It is inevitable — even if it happens on a subconscious level. Allow that impression to settle within you, and let your body respond with a movement of its own.
Note: Let the *dialogue* continue without inviting thought or reflection. Simply remain present and connected to the movements of your body. Emotions may arise — allow them to, without reflecting on them.

Interlude: *Play - Practice - Work*

I cannot emphasise enough that none of the above Interaction exercises should be performed without a certain degree of enjoyment, enthusiasm, interest, or joy — some kind of feeling or energy that elevates the practice from routine and labour to playfulness. For it is only then that the full potential of a specific exercise can unfold.

If you notice, either in yourself or in the group you are facilitating, that the sense of playfulness has disappeared, you need to reframe or reshape the exercise, or perhaps move on to another one. A smooth transition from one exercise to the next is ideal, as this in itself cultivates flexibility and flow.

Exercises should always be carried out with a sense of playfulness — just as work should always be undertaken as a form of practice, with a certain element of playfulness. Otherwise, work will wear down the body or soul, and if it is an exercise, the essence and purpose of the exercise will wither away.

- **Play,** full of playfulness, can only emerge from a sense of freedom and inner motivation.

- All **Practice** must carry within it a trace of playfulness — a lightness that invites exploration.

- Likewise, **Work** must hold space for both playfulness and ongoing practice.

When this balance is neglected, play becomes rigid, practice loses its capacity to foster growth, and work begins to wear down both body and spirit.

Games

About games

The games listed below are just a small selection, but they are among those I have played with thousands of individuals over several decades — both children and adults. I highly recommend the book by **Rudolf Kischnick and Wil van Haren** *(see the literature list)* for more games.

And I repeat: These are the games in which I have observed the best results. A good result, in my view, is when the game influences life beyond the moment of play, particularly in terms of interaction and communication in various forms. The game has then not merely been an isolated moment of fun but has fulfilled its purpose by contributing to a playful, creative, and social life. In a school setting, the difference has been noticeable — both on the same day and in the long-term perspective, spanning several years.

Naturally, the games have been modified, and some have been excluded depending on the age of the participants (ranging from 6 to 75). It is up to your own observations and judgment to decide how and what you choose to implement.

Notes to the School

My advice to teachers has been that children should be allowed to **play and move freely for the first two hours of the day** *(120 minutes or more)* during their first four years of school — in addition to the normally scheduled breaks. Both free spontaneous play and facilitated.

After that for the remainder of their schooling, grade 5 up, they should have at least one hour *(60 minutes or more)* of **play and interactive movement every morning** — in addition to the normally scheduled breaks and hours in physical education and sports.

The so-called "lost" hours will not be missed — quite the opposite, as several studies have shown. These moments of downtime are not wasted; they are essential for children's development in several ways.

Allowing time for rest and play helps to *regulate children's social lives, enhances their cognitive abilities, and supports their mental well-being.* Time spent in non-work activities fosters *creativity, problem-solving, and innovation.* Studies have shown that during moments of relaxation, the brain engages in "mind-wandering," which can lead to unexpected insights and breakthroughs. This is especially true for young children, who benefit from unstructured playtime that allows their brains to process and consolidate information.

Moreover, physical movement and free play are crucial for cognitive function and emotional health. These activities promote neural development, boost focus, and reduce stress. Rather than seeing play as "lost" time, we should recognize its role in boosting overall creativity and well-being. Research consistently supports that when children are given time to rest, play, and interact socially, they return to learning tasks with more focus and improved performance.

This approach requires educators with keen observational skills and a strong sense of intuition, as they must recognize the importance of these hours and incorporate them into a balanced routine. By doing so, they provide students with the necessary foundation for a healthy, creative, and productive life, where learning and well-being are nurtured together.

To the Game Leader

To you who lead the group, I say: always base your approach on observation, not on ideas of how things ought to be or how you had envisioned them. Let your observations then guide you to either:

a) **Allow the activity to continue for as long as the energy remains.** *Many valuable qualities develop simply from letting a game or exercise run its course until it naturally fades out. It will pass through different phases of attention, focus, moods, social tensions, and resolutions. Allowing this to happen helps participants build endurance and the habit of staying present in what is unfolding, rather than "zapping forward" the moment they encounter friction. This strengthens the playfulness ability to "stay in contact."*

b) **Modify the game** by gradually introducing new or alternative rules to make it more engaging, more challenging, calmer, more intense, or to otherwise sustain its life. *This simultaneously cultivates a flexible and creative approach to an ongoing activity. Rules should never function as barbed wire that confines creativity. Rules should only serve as flexible frameworks that create a sense of safety provide direction, and offer inspiration. For this reason, they are always — and should always be — subject to reevaluation.*

c) ***Transition to another game or exercise.*** *Never let the shift to a new activity leave the impression that the participants "failed" at the previous one. Instead, maintain an unspoken attitude of: "Now we are finished with that, and therefore we move on to the next." Ensure that the transition is smooth, positively charged, and forward-oriented in spirit.*

Rule-based Movement Games

"Fox and Hare"

The group stands (standing is important!) in a circle.

One person is chosen to be the hare, another to be the fox. Both wear blindfolds. The fox must catch the hare. Once this happens, they are separated, and the game restarts with reversed roles. When they have finished, **they** choose two new participants.

Variation: The fox and the hare each carry something that makes a sound, such as a small bell. They decide themselves when to use it — to add to the "drama."

- **Important!** Those standing around the circle are *alert* guardians, ensuring that the fox and the hare do not end up outside the circle (and possibly hurt themselves). **Note!** They do not hold hands but move freely within their section of the circle, ready to form a "wall" to prevent the players from going beyond the boundary.

Upgrade 1: The same as above, but the participants keep their eyes open without using their sight. They must still behave and move as if they cannot see their opponent. Naturally, it is up to them how the "drama" unfolds and when it comes to an end. The drama is created intentionally.

- **Upgrade 2**: The same as above, but instead of a large protective circle, both the fox and the hare have their own semicircle of protectors to keep them from getting hurt. The protectors follow their respective animal through the room. The hare's and the fox's protectors avoid touching their animal except when necessary. This variant requires a high level of coordination within the semicircle.

”Dragon Tag”

Everyone spreads out and closes their eyes. The game leader secretly selects 1—4 dragons (depending on the size of the group). The game leader then instructs everyone to open their eyes and start walking around. The chosen dragons also move around but do not reveal themselves or tag anyone yet.

Suddenly, the game leader shouts, **"The dragon has arrived!"** at which point all dragons begin chasing the others. When a dragon tags someone, they say **"Freeze!"** and the tagged player must stop and stand still with their legs apart.

Anyone except the dragons can *free* a frozen player by crawling through their legs. The game continues until everyone has been frozen. However, if there are many active *freers* among the players, the dragons may never win. If this happens, the game can be paused and restarted with fewer dragons.

”A third person in the wind"

Two people always stand behind each other, and together with the other pairs, they form a double circle. One pair is selected — one becomes the runner, and the other the chaser. If the runner stands in front of a pair, the person at the back becomes the new runner. If the runner is tagged, the roles switch, meaning the runner now becomes the chaser.

”Rabies"

The same setup as above, but with the difference that the runner can choose to stand behind a pair instead. When this happens, the person at the front of the pair becomes the new chaser and starts chasing the former chaser, who now takes on the role of the runner.

"Nessie"

Everyone stands in a circle with their eyes closed. The game leader moves around the circle and secretly selects one person to be the *"Head of the Snake."* Then, everyone begins searching for the Snake while keeping their eyes closed. The Snake is the only one with open eyes, moving freely around the room — without chasing or avoiding others. When someone bumps into another person, they whisper: *"Are you the Snake?"* The Snake answers "Yes," while everyone else answers "No." If someone meets the Snake and hears "Yes," they place their hands on the Snake's shoulders and follow them through the room. As more people join, the Snake grows longer. Everyone who becomes part of the Snake must also answer "Yes!" when asked. If someone encounters the Snake, they must first carefully feel their way to the end of the line before opening their eyes. When everyone has joined, the Snake forms a circle, and the game resets. The game leader then selects a new "Head of the Snake."

"Indian Warrior"

One person is the chaser, another is the runner. The rest form a circle but do not hold hands. The rule is as follows: the runner may weave in and out of the circle freely, but the chaser may only exit the circle. To re-enter, the chaser must tag someone in the circle with a tap on the back. The tagged person then becomes the new chaser, while the previous chaser takes their spot in the circle. If the runner is tagged, the roles switch, and the chaser becomes the runner.

- Upgrade: The chaser is not allowed to enter or exit the circle at will. Instead, they must pass on the chasing role to someone else both when the runner enters and exits the circle.

Exercises for Dynamics and Intuition

On Dynamics

In order to work creatively with dynamics so that Interaction and Presence can not only survive but thrive and evolve, one must first become familiar with the dynamic polarities — the tools that one must learn to handle. Equally important is the ability to open up one's *intuitive* capacity. It is through intuition that these tools, these polarities, can be managed effectively.

Dynamics bring life and energy. Dynamics are life in motion. And it is only through intuition that one can, so to speak, manage dynamics in real time.

It is one thing to plan one's day, one's week, and one's time in a way that allows for dynamics, for breath, for a good biological rhythm between wakefulness and sleep, activity and rest. This is, of course, crucial and can have a profound impact on health, energy levels, mood, and creativity. However, when standing in the midst of life, confronted with a situation, a relationship, or a material, the ability to *intuitively* create dynamics becomes essential — because every situation is, in its essence, unique.

Dynamic Polarities in Action

Before anything else, become familiar with the dynamic polarities as I have described them in the first part of the book:

- **Chaos—Structure**

- **Stillness—Wildness**

- **On—Off**

Get to know them in depth, one by one. Then, explore them in relation to their respective polarity.

Individual Movement Exercises for Dynamics

1. **Meditation on a Dynamic Quality**

   o   Sit down and meditate for about ten minutes on a chosen quality, such as **Chaos**. Keep reflections, judgments, and conclusions at bay.

   o   Allow an image of chaos to emerge within you — a moving image, perhaps with colours. This image may be abstract or concrete; it could be a landscape in motion.

   o   Let this image fill you, feel it within your body. Allow it to become intense and as vivid as possible. Let it transform into bodily sensations and emotions within you.

2.   Embodiment through Movement

○   Stand up and allow this inner image and feeling of chaos to take hold of your body and set it in motion.

○   Your body becomes filled with a chaotic movement quality.

○   Dance and move freely for about 10—15 minutes, guided by the quality and the sensations you experience in your body.

3.   Stillness and Reflection

○   Sit down again and let stillness return to your body.

○   However allow the feeling of chaos to remain as a lingering echo within.

○   Simply experience and observe for about 10 minutes.

4.   Repetition and Expansion

○   Repeat these three steps multiple times with the same element.

○   With each new repetition, avoid falling into routine. Instead, explore how your experience of chaos in body and movement expands, evolves, and offers new sensations and insights.

Carry out this four-step process with each individual dynamic element.

Group Movement Exercises for Dynamics

*If you are working in a group, follow the same step-by-step process. However, in the beginning, the exercises should be performed **in parallel, rather than interactively**. The mere fact that you are practicing in the same space will enhance the experience.*

Once participants begin to develop a **bodily awareness of the dynamic elements**, you can gradually introduce interaction:

1.   Initially, the group chooses a **shared dynamic element** to explore.

2.   As the practice develops, each participant selects their own element and allows it to interact with those of others.

———————————

Dynamic Processes

Individual Dynamic Process Exercise

1. Practise **gradual transitions** between an element and its polarity.

2. In your initial meditation, focus on the element you will begin with — for example, **Stillness**.

3. Gradually introduce the **opposite element**, in this case, **Wildness**, in your mind.

4. Let go of the image and allow your body's movement to **follow this process**, shifting from Stillness to Wildness in a gradual and conscious way.

5. Finally, sit down again, return to stillness, and let the experience of this transition remain within you.

Follow the same approach with the other dynamic elements — moving **from one element to its polarity**.

Group Dynamic Process Exercise

If practicing in a group, follow the steps outlined above, but now with **dynamic processes** as the focus of the exercise.

Experiencing the Scale of Intensity

Experimenting with the **scale of intensity**, that is, the gradual transition from extreme **On** through a balanced midpoint to extreme **Off**, is a powerful way to develop an understanding of dynamics within the polarity of On — Off.

A highly effective way to grasp the **scale of intensity** is to explore the **seven levels of tension**, an approach developed by the French actor and pedagogue **Jacques Lecoq**. These exercises were a fundamental part of the training at his theatre school in Paris, **École Internationale de Théâtre Jacques Lecoq**.

The Seven Levels of Tension are:

1. **Catatonic (A Jellyfish Washed Ashore)**
   No tension whatsoever. The body is limp, barely able to move.

2. **Relaxed (Californian)**
   Very "laid back," with minimal tension in the body.

3. **Neutral (Present)**
   Efficient. A perfect balance between tension and relaxation.

4. **Alert (Curious)**
   Light tension in the body, heightened awareness, looking around attentively.

5. **Suspense ("Is there a threat in the room?")**
   A significant amount of tension in the body, preparing for action.

6. **Passionate ("There is a threat in the room!")**
   Intense tension, a state of urgency, panic, or strong emotion.

7. **Tragic ("The bomb is about to explode!")**
   Maximum tension — petrified, completely frozen, holding breath.

Exploring the Seven Levels of Tension

Step 1: Individual Exploration

1. Catatonic (Jellyfish)

- Lie down or collapse into a seated position.

- Feel the weight of your body sinking, completely slack and lifeless.

- If standing, allow your body to hang without any control or structure.

- Move minimally — slowly, without direction or intention.

2. Relaxed (Californian)

- Slowly rise to a standing position and begin moving gently.

- Imagine walking along a warm beach, feeling carefree and unhurried.

- Let your arms sway loosely, releasing any unnecessary tension.

3. Neutral (Present)

- Stand in a balanced, upright posture.

- Feel your body alert but neither tense nor slack.

- Move with ease and efficiency, as though carrying out a purposeful task.

4. Alert (Curious)

- Sharpen your gaze and lightly activate your body.

- Start looking around as if searching for something.

- Feel a slight tension in your muscles, as though you are ready to react.

- Make small, tentative movements — like a young animal discovering its surroundings.

5. Suspense ("Is there a threat in the room?")

- Heighten your senses further.

- Notice your breathing becoming shorter, your shoulders possibly lifting slightly.

- Move cautiously, as if trying to sneak or avoid detection.

- Feel your muscles preparing for a possible flight or fight response.

6. Passionate ("There is a threat in the room!")

- The tension escalates to an intense level.

- React instinctively — run, hide, shout, or physically express the emotion.

- Let your body take full control of your movement.

- Feel your heartbeat racing, your body filled with urgent energy.

7. Tragic ("The bomb is about to explode!")

- Suddenly stop and become completely still.

- Feel an overwhelming tension running through your entire body.

- Let your hands and face express frozen terror.

- Hold your breath for a moment, then release all tension with a deep exhalation.

Step 2: Transitioning Between Levels

- Begin from **Catatonic** and gradually move through each level until reaching **Tragic**.

- Then, descend back down through the levels in **reverse order**.

- Experiment with **spontaneous transitions** — for example, shifting **directly from Relaxed to Suspense**, or from **Alert to Catatonic**.

- Practise moving between levels **both gradually and abruptly**.

Step 3: Applying the Levels in Improvisation

- ***Partner or Group Work***

  o One person calls out a level, and the others instantly embody that level of tension.

  o Observe how the body and breath adjust accordingly.

- ***Scene Exploration***

  o Create **short scenes** in which characters transition through multiple levels of tension.

  o Example: One character starts in **Relaxed** but suddenly shifts to **Passionate**, while another begins in **Suspense** and drops into **Catatonic**.

  o Discover how tension shifts can **drive a story forward and create dynamic contrast**.

The exercises involving the **seven levels of tension** are an excellent and playful way to develop an awareness of intensities and gain mastery over the **scale of intensity**.

Within the **field of dynamics**, the key question is:

- **At what intensity should I perform this action?**

- **What level of intensity do I want to create?**

Intuition Practise

Before we explore specific exercises to develop intuition, it is important to emphasise that all the interactive exercises described so far also train intuition. This is a key point: *one of the fundamental factors that enables the smooth flow of play, interactive practice, or creative expression is **intuition**.* Intuition is what allows you to take the right action at the right moment. Good timing is the result of intuition.

Developing Your Intuition

To begin with, developing intuition requires trusting the intuitive signals and impulses that arise within you. Intuition always presents itself as an impulse or a piece of information that has a direct pathway to action. If you are not already naturally intuitive — that is, if you are not accustomed to listening to your intuition — these signals and impulses may initially be very subtle.

The first step, then, is to **listen to them** and cultivate a **trust** in the accuracy of these signals. What we commonly refer to as "gut feeling" is actually intuition in action. The best way to develop it is to start small.

Trusting your intuition requires **courage**, but it also requires **awareness and attentiveness** — not only to recognise where your intuition is leading you, but also to observe what happens as a result of following it. What are the consequences of your actions? What effects do your decisions have on your surroundings?

Possible intuitive impulses must, in a sense, be *"washed in the waters of awareness"*. This happens through **presence** and **interaction**. If impulses are not brought into awareness, they remain mere **impulsivity** — and impulsivity, unlike intuition, can often lead to missteps. The difference is like that between *playing with your friends* or *simply messing around*

As I have emphasised many times, presence and interaction form the foundation. These must be approached dynamically through intuition—only then can the timing fall into place, allowing playfulness and creativity to flow endlessly.

However, by **awareness**, I do not mean intellectual reflection, which is often burdened with *judgements, expectations, and preconceived ideas*. By awareness, I simply mean being *awake, attentive, and noticing:*

- What is happening?

- How does it affect those I am interacting with?

- What are the consequences of my actions and decisions?

When we cultivate this type of awareness, our impulses become *refined* — they begin to express themselves more clearly as **true intuition**. Over time, our intuition becomes sharper, and we can live with it and act upon it with increasing confidence.

The Difference Between Intuitive and Isolated Impulses

Impulses that arise when we are **not** present or engaged with the world around us are merely *self-referential*. They have no **living connection** to our surroundings.

However, the impulses that arise when we **are in contact** with and interacting with the world draw their *information from the larger whole* — the very whole of which we ourselves are a part.

This is not a moral judgement against impulses that lack external connection. On the contrary, many people have had their impulsivity or creativity suppressed during childhood (the problem is spelled *school*). For them, the very first step is simply to **reactivate their impulses** — to generate a flow of impulses.

> There are many ways to reignite such a flow. I recommend literature and workshops based on the works of, among others, Anne Bogart, Keith Johnstone, and Julia Cameron, as well as those offered within the contact improvisation community. (See literature list)

However, the next step is to *align our impulses with the larger whole*, allowing them to be guided by intuition rather than mere instinct. This is particularly crucial when engaging in interaction with others, and even more so when working with children.

Even though this approach requires you to step out of the centre, you will experience yourself as profoundly **creative** —

perhaps even more so than before. The difference is that *this creativity remains in constant contact with the larger context,* the bigger picture.

Furthermore, this form of creativity has a far **wider sphere of inspiration** than a creativity that is confined only to **one's personal, individual domain**.

Exercises to Develop Intuition

The foundation of intuitive practice lies in **listening to yourself at a deeper level** while simultaneously being **attentive and present** in relation to something external — something in the world around you.

Remember: **intuition does not align with rationality or intellectual analysis**. In fact, intuition not only functions without these but actively requires their absence in order to be heard at all.

Individual Intuition Exercises

1.   *Cultivating Present Awareness*

o   To access your intuition, it is essential to cultivate **presence and attentiveness**.

o   Practices such as **meditation, breathing exercises, and presence exercises** help to quiet everyday mental noise, increases inner peace, and allow you to listen inwards.

o   When your mind is calm, it becomes easier to **perceive and trust your intuitive insights**.

2.   *Attuning to Bodily Sensations*

o   As mentioned earlier, **bodily sensations** can be an important signal of intuition.

o   When faced with a decision or situation, **pay attention** to how your body reacts.

o   Do you feel **tense or relaxed, heavy or light?**

o   These physical signals can provide valuable **insights into your intuitive understanding** of a situation.

3. *Trusting Your Gut Feeling*

- o Learning to **trust** your gut instinct is key, even when you cannot immediately rationalise why you feel a certain way.

- o Over time, you will begin to **differentiate between intuitive gut feelings and those influenced by fear or anxiety**.

- o Building this trust is crucial to strengthening your **intuitive abilities**.

4. *Practicing with Small Decisions*

- o Start by applying intuition to **small everyday choices**, such as:

  - ■ What to eat

  - ■ Which route to take on your way to work or a friend's house

- o Observe how your **intuitive choices feel in your body** and take note of the outcomes.

- o This will gradually help you **build confidence in your intuition**.

5. *Pausing and Reflecting*

- o   In **stressful situations**, it can be difficult to hear your intuition.

- o   Taking a **moment to pause, breathe, and reflect** gives your **intuitive mind the space it needs** to provide guidance.

Through these exercises, intuition shifts from being a vague, occasional hunch to becoming a reliable, natural, and ever-present guide in daily life and creative practice.

Group Intuition Exercises

Here follows a collection of interaction exercises in pairs or groups that primarily build on intuition and develop the same. It can be difficult to understand how intuition develops from the physical exercises described. But this is not something you need to worry about. Decades of experience with these very exercises have confirmed that this is indeed the case. All I can say is that it has to do with balancing the body's directions in the space, how the psyche relates to its own body and to the surroundings, and how actively interactive movement work relates to inner peace.

Blindfolded Leading

These exercises are performed in pairs. One person keeps their eyes closed while the other, with their eyes open, takes on the role of the guide. (blindfolds are not necessary but can sometimes be a help in accepting "not-looking")

""Blind Pair Running"

The sighted partner leads the blindfolded one through the room. The guide maintains a parallel position and holds a firm grip on the blindfolded partner. Movement can range from walking to jogging, or even short bursts of fast running. It may also involve walking

backwards. The manner of touch can also vary — from a firm and clear grip to subtle directional cues through light touches.

The guide must never push or force the blindfolded person into a higher speed but should move in close connection with their comfort level, which is usually linked to their courage and their ability to surrender to the leadership of the guide.

The essence of this exercise lies with the blindfolded participant. They must allow their body to be led, letting their legs move on their own while maintaining complete inner calm — *as if leaning against a wall in a state of rest*. This is what makes the exercise challenging.

"Blind Back Guidance"
This is also done in pairs. The sighted partner places a hand between the blindfolded person's shoulder blades. The blindfolded participant moves backward, walking towards the guide's hand.

The blindfolded person determines the speed and challenges their own limits in this regard. However, it is the guide who navigates through the space. A light touch between the shoulder blades is sufficient for the blindfolded participant to understand whether they should move left or right.

The sighted partner should not focus their gaze on the back of their partner but instead let their eyes rest on the room ahead, observing the space, the direction they are moving in, and the position of other pairs or obstacles.

The core of the exercise lies in the blindfolded participant's ability to, on the one hand, set their own speed according to their courage, and on the other hand, maintain relaxation in their arms, shoulders, neck, and jaw while preserving an inner sense of calm and peace. In this exercise, **determination** (expressed through the setting of speed) is balanced against **surrender** (entrusting the direction to the guide).

"Blind Sounding Guidance"

In pairs. In this exercise, too, the blindfolded person moves backwards towards their partner, setting their own pace. However, the guide does not use physical contact but instead relies solely on their voice. The guide may choose to sing on a single note, hum, or pronounce isolated words.

To add complexity, the guide can introduce moments of silence, move to different spots in the room, and vocalise from a new location. This creates silent intervals in which the blindfolded participant must *reach out into the space with their perception* to locate their guide. Surprisingly, this exercise can be performed with multiple pairs in the same room, as we have an exceptional ability to recognise and distinguish sounds.

The essence of this exercise lies in how the blindfolded participant *extends their listening backwards*, expanding their auditory perception throughout the space.

”Blind Object Exchange”

The group stands in a circle. One person steps into the centre, holding an object. As soon as they enter, they close their eyes. A second person then enters the circle, also blindfolded. Without using sound, they must find one another, and the object must be transferred from one to the other.

Once the first person has passed on the object, they open their eyes and choose another participant to enter the circle blindfolded and receive the object.

To make the exercise more challenging, the person selecting the new participant can place them on the opposite side of the circle and spin them around a few times before allowing them to begin searching for the person holding the object.

The Labyrinth Games

Preparation: A large floor area is needed. Furniture or other objects should be placed strategically to form corridors or pathways.

Basic Rules:

1. Participants must move through these corridors at a steady pace — not too slowly, but not running either.

2. Once a person enters a corridor, they must follow it to the end; they may not change direction midway.

3. Participants may not deliberately follow another person.

Variation 1: "Avoid Meeting"

Three people move through the labyrinth, trying to avoid a *frontal encounter*. Crossing paths is permitted, but if two participants face each other head-on, they must exit the labyrinth. Immediately, two new participants take their places. There are always three people moving within the labyrinth at any given time. Strive for a calm flow.

Variant 2: "Meeting"

As in Variant 1, three people move freely within the labyrinth. However, at the cue ***"From now on,"*** all three must attempt to meet simultaneously in the centre of the labyrinth, approaching from three different directions. This must be done without significantly altering the speed of their movement. Strive for a calm flow.

"Exact Mirror"

A pair stands opposite each other. They have agreed on who will lead and who will follow. The leader makes movements with their arms, and the follower imitates them simultaneously and as exactly as a mirror. The exercise is for the leader to perform the movements so

slowly and simply that from the outside, it is impossible to tell who is leading. The leader should give themselves the feeling of being inside the other person's arms, leading them from within the follower. The follower should give themselves the feeling that the leader is inside their arms and that they can completely hand over the movement of their arms to the leader.

Upgrade: The group leader calls out when the pair should switch roles. When this happens, the transition from follower to leader and vice versa should not be visible. The leader will ask them to switch more frequently, from once a minute down to once every five seconds. Finally, the leader will ask them to both lead and follow at the same time.

"Blind Mirror"

The pair stands opposite each other. The setup is the same as in *Exact Mirror*, but this time it is done with eyes closed. The concept is still the exact mirror, but now it cannot be corrected by sight. Intuition must be used. The goal is not for it to be perfect or identical. The goal is the attempt and the special effort.

"Through the Circle, Leap"

Everyone is positioned in a circle. The circle moves quite quickly around. The group leader calls out a number. The number refers to how many people are to run across to the other side. The participants who feel an impulse to run do so, crossing the circle. They follow the impulse that arises in their bodies. The group leader might call out 6! and immediately 8 people feel the impulse to run. This should not be considered wrong, but simply as a fact. The important thing is that those who ran followed their impulse. The group leader might call out 0! and 3 people run. She calls 9! and 9 people run. Both situations are just as valid as the other. The point is that you hear a number and, instead of wanting to do the right thing, you must listen to the impulses of your body. There is also the moment where perhaps 12 people suddenly run across the circle without colliding. Again, it is intuition that saves everyone from colliding. There is no time to calculate. The body handles the intelligence that prevents confrontation.

Finally: Improvisation in General

All improvisation, whether in theatre, movement/dance, voice/song, or music, trains ***intuition.*** Through its lack of a plan, choreography, or composed arrangement, and its open interaction, it forces presence into action to solve problems. *Only intuition can provide solutions to problems that need to be solved in the very second they arise.*

PART 3

the child's play
and its
significance
in Adult Life

The Childs Play and
its Significance in Adult Life

Here follows a categorisation of forms of play, based on observations of children's play. Various categorisations can be found within play research, and studies have also explored which types of skills emerge from different forms of play—something I have also investigated.

For each form of play, I also examine the question:
how does a particular form of play
manifest in adult life?

What does an adult's life look like if they have not had the opportunity to develop the specific skills that a particular form of play offers? And what is needed?

⁻ *The Pre-Play Stage*

The pre-play stage involves exploring the physical environment and discovering what exists, both materially and psychologically. It is a sensory and perceptual understanding of one's surroundings, their context, and the components.

- *What can I find here?*

- *What is happening here?*

- *How does it feel?*

- *What is possible right now, in this place and with this material?*

The pre-play stage is an orientation and examination of both physical and psychological facts, and it broadly corresponds to the initial phase of a Childs play-life.

At this stage, the infant instinctively explores its movement possibilities and the materials it encounters. During this phase, observation, perception, and cognition develop. Here, the foundation is laid for the emerging ability to assess and make decisions in relation to a material.

This can involve purely material facts, where the child first "listens" to the material, getting acquainted with it before interacting with and using it. If the pre-play stage is skipped in a social context, the one who enters may be perceived as an insensitive elephant barging into an ongoing situation. Such an elephant will struggle to connect with what is already present— an already manifested structure of social life or an ongoing creative process.

To participate effectively, *a certain amount of time* in the pre-play stage is always required: a time to land in the situation. **One must "tune" oneself, adjust one's instrument, before diving into the context.**

In the pre-play stage of a social situation, there is also what is called the ***"play signal",*** an invitation or query to play, whether verbal or otherwise. One needs affirmation from those with whom they wish to play. This may appear in various forms. For example, with dogs, play signals are very clear, such as extending the front paws, chin to the ground, and tail up—or a gentle touch with the paw of the one making the invitation.

Adults' participation in children's play

Among adults, one often sees a less than ideal habit of clumsily entering children's play in an insensitive manner, which is frequently an expression of a well-meaning but control-driven need. We tend to wish to steer the play so that it is fair, safe, educational, or otherwise "good." But the risk is that we disrupt and hinder the play, *preventing the participants from developing the necessary skills through the play itself.* This also provides a poor example for children, something they may later replicate in their own play by controlling, directing, or criticizing their peers. This ultimately stifles playfulness.

Play, therefore, requires a sensitive pre-play stage. Adults can, of course, join in or invite children to play, but they bear the greatest responsibility **to tone themselves down, to "tune in" with others, and to be receptive.** An optimally playful play has no fixed leader but roles that shift according to the play's own logic and needs, not according to rank or status. Animals, especially dogs, wolves, and monkeys, offer models here, as they set aside status, rank, strength, and speed, adapting to the group and to the other participants. This ensures that the play continues and remains as rewarding as possible.

The Pre-Play Stage in the Adult World

As adults, we must be more diligent in our pre-play if we are to create playfulness in our lives. We must make space for it. It involves attuning ourselves and asking:

- *What can I find here?*

- *What is happening here?*

- *What "materials" can I choose to engage with?*

- *How does this material feel?*

- *How can I contribute?*

- *Do I need to ask a question?*

- *Do I need to invite someone or something in?*

- *What is the right question that opens the door to interaction?*

- *What rules apply here and now?*

If I wish to "play" at work, interact with my colleagues, my colours, my tones, or my friends, I must leave rank and status at the door. Whether I am the boss or a subordinate, I must neutralize that status, attune to the same level as others or the material, and focus instead on the facts—what is there to know after I have asked myself these internal questions. What my role becomes in the interaction will be determined by the interaction itself. Without giving time to this pre-play stage, there can be no playfulness, and thus no optimal situation.

By sensitively considering the psychological and spatial situation, one can connect more effectively and more easily enter into interaction—whether it concerns people or materials.

- *Social Body Play*

This is often referred to in play literature as *"Rough and Tumble Play".*

*You will also find it under the name **"Original Play"**—a form that Fred Donaldson presents as the primordial play he has discovered through studying and engaging in play with animals, in which young children naturally participate in a similar manner.*

It is also called *sensory-motor play*, for its defining feature is the coordination of muscles and senses as participants move and interact. Through this form of play, sensory and motor development integrates seamlessly with the individual's impulses. Certain actions and movement patterns repeat, becoming tied to positive sensations — joy, excitement, curiosity, and the like.

This process holds profound significance for an individual's motor development and relationship with their body. When positive feelings and perceptions anchor one's connection to the body, they stabilise a deeper sense of belonging and coherence within oneself.

Animals

This is also the most common form of play among animals. According to the Zoologist Gordon Burghardt, it is observed not only in mammals but also in reptiles, fish, and birds. Significant research has explored "non-functional" behavior in animals — actions that serve no purpose other than the act itself. In other words, the goal of these actions exists solely within the play.

This type of play is most developed in wolves, dogs, and apes. Among these species, we find play elements such as:

- *Play signals*

- *Role reversals*

- *Self-handicapping*

- *Rule-breaking followed by apologies*

The way animals play can teach us much, particularly regarding ***self-handicapping*** — a behaviour often adopted by the stronger, faster, or higher-ranked individual in a group.

During play, such individuals intentionally make themselves weaker, slower, or set aside their social rank to create balance between the participants. Through this, play becomes more reciprocal. This ensures that the exchange of actions and forces remains balanced, enabling the play to continue without interruption from someone "winning."

Hunter-Gatherer Cultures

Developmental psychologist Peter Gray and his team conducted a meta-study of anthropological research on authentic, still-living hunter-gatherer cultures, focusing on play and learning. Gray's findings revealed similar patterns among children and adolescents in these societies. Their play could go on endlessly due to the practice of *self-handicapping.* Winning was not the objective; instead, *the driving force was the generation of energy and joy.* Learning and the development of sensory-motor skills were welcomed side effects. The goal of the play was for everyone to have fun. Play should not be a battle, even if it may appear like one, as long as the battle is part of a specific playful dynamic. Play should be a dynamic flow, and when it is, it is optimal.

In social body play, bodily and emotional tensions are released. The fundamental needs for *touch, bodily warmth, and the exchange of energy* are fulfilled. Along with these, the deeply important and foundational *sense of connection, coherence and belonging is built* on an experiential, emotional, and action-oriented level.

Body Awareness and Self-Esteem

Through this type of play, body awareness develops — an understanding of where one's weight is, the center of balance, the boundaries of one's skin, limbs, and body. It also fosters an awareness of *personal and shared physical boundaries:* where my body ends and yours begins; where my strength or yours is too much or too little. Balance, strength, and self-directed movement are constantly challenged and refined.

Here, the bodily foundation for developing self-esteem is laid.

If play were structured around winners and losers, only self-confidence would develop, and only in a select few — the winners, the stronger, smarter, steadier, and tougher individuals. Since winning is not the purpose of play, self-esteem can develop freely, rooted in bodily self-awareness and the experience of joy and strength in one's own body. This builds a stable sense of being valuable, regardless of performance. And, as author and psychologist Jesper Juul points out, **genuine self-esteem cannot**

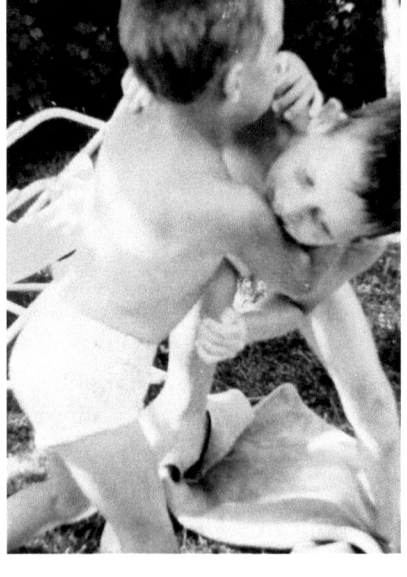

develop from self-confidence alone. *Conversely, confidence in one's abilities and actions can easily grow from a well-rooted sense of self-worth.*

> ***Self-esteem*** *is more about how you **feel** about yourself as a person and whether you value your own worth. It's foundational to your emotional well-being and influences how you handle failure, criticism, or success.*

> ***Self-confidence*** *is about your belief in your **abilities** in specific situations. You can have high self-confidence in one area (e.g., public speaking) but still struggle with low self-esteem, feeling unworthy or inadequate overall.*

Among dogs and wolves, as mentioned, we also find play signals, role reversals, and rule-breaking followed by apologies. Play signals are the invitations to engage. Play cannot be forced; it depends on a voluntary and self-motivated decision. For this reason, invitations or questions — ones that leave room for both a "yes" and a "no" — are necessary.

Roles and flexibility

Role shifting involve adapting one's function to the context of the moment. No role is ever fixed. *Roles shift depending on what occurs or what is mutually agreed upon.* In social body play, such agreements are not typically verbal but rather tacit understandings: ***"Let's make this work for everyone."***

This mindset nurtures an inner flexibility regarding what one needs to be in relation to the other: *initiator, follower, the stronger (in play), the weaker, the observer, or the one fully immersed in play. (In fantasy-based play, roles tend to become more specific.)* This may sound overly intellectual or conscious when written about, but in practice, it develops organically within the friction and interaction of play. ***One finds one's place, role, and function in the moment, guided by intuition.***

This process works as long as the individual — whether animal, child, or adult — is, in a broader sense, **well-fed, safe, and healthy.** Otherwise, factors like insecurity, anger, or a need to retaliate or dominate may disrupt the play, diminishing its playful essence and purpose.

Adults' participation in children's play

As mentioned, playfulness is the core, the purpose, and the life of play. This is where an older child, an adult, or another responsible individual may step in. They can act as *catalysts or correctives, addressing emotions, excessive force, inflexibility, or insecurity.* They may, for instance, provide a *"space"* within the play for these elements
— a resistance, a channeling.

This resembles the approach of an Aikido master who meets an incoming force, not with counterforce, but by absorbing and redirecting it. In this way, *rigidity is captured and transformed into movement,* and insecurity, no matter how it manifests, can be met with the needed softness, patience, or clarity.

Among animals, however, the process is often less forgiving. An individual that repeatedly disrupts play by misusing strength or neglecting to pause and "apologize" is excluded. Such individuals typically struggle socially overall and may be ostracized from the group — a devastating fate for most social species.

For humans, too, *the need to belong* is fundamental to both mental and physical health. Exclusion often leads to profound harm, sometimes fatal. Play has likely always been both a self-fulfilling form of interaction and a way of learning how to function together in a group.

Social Intelligence

Through the simple, fundamental physical interactions of play, social intelligence naturally develops—the ability to sense what one can, may, or should do in a given situation. This forms the foundation for being oneself in social settings. It takes shape through physical experience, spatial awareness, and the deep confidence that arises from bodily memory, lived experience, and the sense of feeling at home in one's own body.

As emotions and personal needs colour these interactions, play fosters the management of them. Participants must adapt their own needs to others'. *A one-sided, self-centered domination of the play would quickly extinguish the joy and connection.*

Through physical exchanges — the rough, chaotic interaction — what disrupts or undermines play is gradually refined. Everyone, after all, wants the play to continue indefinitely. Everyone, I would argue, carries an internal vision of what play could be and what is needed for it to thrive. **What is required is time.** It must be practiced (without being goal-oriented) and allowed to settle into every fiber of the body.

Play hones the child, rather than the child playing to hone themselves. A child's reason for playing lies solely in the positive experience it brings. There is no motivation beyond that. While external motives such as maintaining social status or proving strength may exist, they detract from playfulness, shorten the duration of play, and diminish its joy.

This original form of play provides the best foundation for developing social intelligence.

Infants

A precursor to this type of play is found in the interaction between parent and infant. Laboratory studies using EEG have shown that when parent and child engage in eye contact and simple movements, touch and vocalisations, their brain frequencies synchronise. They enter a state of psychological and neurological resonance.

This reveals yet another dimension of our fundamental need — and innate ability — *to connect, to bond, to exist in relation.* As mentioned, both our mental and physical health depend on this sense of belonging: *the feeling of being part of a meaningful whole.*

The Fundamental Forces

In social body play, we find the elements of movement and force: *push — pull — follow — stop* (where stopping or holding applies only to one's own movement, not restraining others).

Adults with other adults

*As adults, interacting with others, we must always be mindful of the boundaries of the other person, our own boundaries and when, metaphorically, we need to **push or pull, follow or stop** — and to what extent.*

These elements are ever-present in interaction, typically on a mental and social level rather than a physical one. Playfulness can only emerge when they occur with respect for the other's integrity, free will, and motivation.

Children who experience these elements in play and grow accustomed to handling them find it easier as adults to manage them in their abstract psychological forms. Similarly, adults given a chance to practice these elements anew through play — learning to balance *push, pull, follow, and stop* — gain greater potential for connection and joy. It can be done within the framework of dance, play and group exercises.

All interactions contain these elements. They reveal boundaries — our own and others'. In play, boundaries are not barriers or constraints; they define the space within which one moves, dances, and plays freely. In play boundaries are the framework for freedom.

The bodily, sensorimotor experience of something often lays the foundation for, and sometimes makes possible, its psychological counterpart.

- The Interactive Movement and Rule-Based Play

Origin

The interactive movement- or rule-based game is a fundamental expression of human creativity and interaction, accompanying humanity for thousands of years. Its roots can be traced back to religious ceremonies and initiation rites of the mysteries, which over time also found their way into the streets and became accessible to "ordinary" people. One can still find the ritual structure today in certain circle dances, such as those we maintain around the Christmas tree and the Midsummer pole. Many rule-based games also retain these original elements, such as: what is permitted and what is forbidden; when one must stand still and when movement is allowed again; when and how one can be freed; how movement together and cooperation should or can take place; what the ultimate goal is and how the game comes to an end.

But where did sports like hockey and football come from? They are play-based rule games as well, aren't they?

*All the structured, competitive ball games that exist today were once spontaneous, in-the-moment games played by people in hunter-gatherer societies, carried out with **no interest in winning**—only for the joy of playing together. This still exists in those cultures today, but if you look around, you may also find it in your own neighborhood. People engage with the ball for the sake of interaction and satisfaction—something they can do together.*

When we became agriculturalists around 10,000 years ago and divided into families struggling for their own survival, the element of competition emerged: families against families; villages against villages; individuals against individuals. In hunter-gatherer cultures, there were and are no internal conflicts, as these societies are based on autonomy and the sharing of resources—whether child or adult. This applies to almost all hunter-gatherer communities, whether in South America, Africa, or Asia. In agricultural societies, however, a culture of coercion and violence emerged, linked to a family's survival. Rule-based games then developed into competitions, becoming arenas where individuals could assert their strength in relation to others through physical contests such as football, wrestling, etc.—a way to establish dignity through achievement — at least emotionally and temporarily.

Later, as people moved into cities during industrialization, ball games needed to be regulated even further out of necessity, leading to the construction of designated playing fields. Eventually, arenas were built to accommodate spectators who were not playing but passionately following those who were. Most ball games—such as rugby, football, cricket, croquet, and many more—originate from the nation that underwent the most extensive industrialization: Great Britain.

Characteristics

The movement- or rule-based game is about interacting through movement and activity within set frameworks and rules, where the focus is on what we perceive with our senses, how we use our bodies, the movement itself, and how we engage with others. Examples of this type of play include traditional *chasing games, hide-and-seek, team games,* and many more.

What makes this form of play so significant is not only the joy and movement it brings but also what happens beneath the surface. Within the play itself, there is a continuous practice of skills essential both for individual development and for navigating social environments. *Here, we develop cooperation and problem solving, reciprocity, mutuality, attentiveness, and the ability to respond to the moment. We also refine motor and cognitive agility, making both the body and the mind more fluid and adaptable.*

But it is more than physical, cognitive and social training. This type of play also prepares us to intuitively navigate the three vital elements: **presence, interaction, and dynamics.** When we play, we learn to be present in the now, to relate to others with flexibility and sensitivity, and to follow the rhythm and flow of the game. An internal adjustment takes place. And, often without even realising it, *we develop a natural flexibility toward the rules of interaction—and toward one another—in a way that is both functional and balanced.*

The Role of Rules and Agreements

A special dimension of this type of play lies in the relationship with rules and agreements. *Through play, we come to understand* **rules as more than mere limitations.** We begin to see them as foundational structures *that make certain experiences possible.* Without rules, a game like hide-and-seek or football would become something entirely different; the framework creates the **space** in which specific experiences can be brought to life.

Rules can be explicit—as in team games—but they can also be subtle and implicit or even embedded in the environment itself. For example, a game may be defined by *the natural conditions* of its setting, such as a garden with its bushes and hiding spots, or by the props at hand, like a ball or a rope.

Joyful Practice—The Paradoxical Nature of Play

At the heart of all play is its spontaneous emergence and intrinsic motivation. It is joyful, creative, and self-sustaining. We do not play to achieve something specific or to consciously practice skills. Instead, it is the opposite: we play because we want to play, and as a natural consequence of this, the play shapes us.

This is the paradoxical nature of play—it is at once entirely free and deeply formative.

When we play, we are fully present in the moment. We follow the flow of the play, and in that movement, *we develop effortlessly.* It is also in this state—where we are *not driven* by performance or goal-oriented ambition—that the most *authentic and creative* forms of play emerge. **The optimal play is one that is purely playful, where we meet the present moment with curiosity and engagement.**

But how can a game like football or ice hockey, which is so deeply rooted in the desire to win, still capture the essence of play and foster the development of all these essential abilities—including the joy of playing together? The answer is simple: by letting go of the motive to win. Releasing the desire for victory and focusing solely on the present moment, where true presence resides, and on the interplay with teammates. That is what leads to success—as a byproduct.

To place one's presence in the future, in the anticipated victory, is detrimental to performance *because it weakens the very interaction that is essential in all sports (even non-team sports). This has been demonstrated time and again and is widely acknowledged in martial arts, sport climbing, athletics, and team sports alike. It is counterproductive to be mentally anywhere other than the here and now. If one is driven by the need to "succeed" or "win" and has part of their awareness locked onto the desired outcome, they risk missing the subtleties of the moment—losing their grip on the climbing hold, mistiming a pass of the boll, or failing to anticipate an opponent's uppercut.*

Adults, Rules and Play

For the adult, interactive movement and rule-based play can be seen as a reflection of life itself. Play becomes a metaphor for social interaction and for the myriad small and large rules that govern our lives. Just as in play, in life we must navigate between boundaries and freedom, between the individual and the collective, between the predictable and the unexpected.

Participating in social contexts as an adult involves constant negotiation with these forces and boundaries. It is about developing and maintaining an inner movement and flexibility —the ability to adapt to changes without becoming stuck, to meet others with Reciprocity, and to adjust to the dynamics of each situation.

From Play to Playfulness

Here, what develops into playfulness is not merely something fun or childlike but an essential life skill. It teaches us to be creative in our relationships, to balance our own needs with those of others, and to find joy, meaning, and opportunity within the rules and structures that might otherwise feel limiting.

Through playfulness, we learn to see *structures, frameworks and rules as an opportunity for interaction rather than a burden.*

Let me once again quote Viktor Frankl:
"Everything can be taken from a man but one thing—the last of the human freedoms: to choose one's attitude in any given set of circumstances."

227

Playfulness as the Core of Life's Quality

When we truly tap into our inner freedom and approach the world with playfulness and creativity, we connect more deeply with both ourselves and others in ways that foster growth and flourishing.

In playful interaction—whether through movement, creative expression, or social exchange—we discover the possibility of living in balance with ourselves and those around us. It is in this space that the new, the unexpected, and the vital can emerge.

Playfulness and creativity breaks patterns, creates openness, and helps us adapt to life's constant flow. It also gives us the courage to face the world with an open heart and a flexible attitude.

And perhaps most importantly, it reminds us that life is not just meant to be endured but to be lived and loved.

- *The Fantasy Play*

In fantasy play, a personal interaction takes place with two worlds simultaneously: the sensory reality—its form, nature, and possibilities as a means of expression—and the inner world of sensations, emotions, images, and thoughts. The motivation stems from *the need to process and express impressions*—experiences and perceptions that have created some form of imbalance—a kind of self-regulation.

The play originates from a personal need for manifestation (from the Latin *Manifestare*: to make apparent). The material that takes form through personal expression is the result of an ongoing process of assimilation—the internal processing and integration of experiences, impressions, and emotions. In the act of *playing* itself, the processing, expression, and manifestation occur simultaneously.

Fantasy (from the Greek *Phainō*: to bring forth, to make appear) means that what lives inside the child becomes visible, tangible, and thus possible to process. It can be something as simple as an emotion, but it can also involve more complex inner or outer conflicts or even traumas.
The processing through play happens intuitively. This means that the fantasizing, creative, and playful individual, through their action, knows what to do as they are doing it. The starting points of the process, that which needs to be resolved, are often unconscious. Instead, awareness revolves around the interaction

with the material that manifests the processed inner world. In contrast to a cognitive process, one might call it *a dream-like form of processing in action.*

In fantasy play, both the ability to feel and experience emotions and *the capacity to perceive what happens internally* —through images, sensations, and impulses—are developed, along with *the ability to process and work through these experiences.* Additionally, there is *the training of perception and grasping the physical possibilities available*, as well as *the ability to express the inner world externally* so that it becomes visible and/or audible.

The inner world is manifested in words, song, movement, building, sculpting, and so on. What matters is not so much the final product as the very process of fantasizing and manifesting.

The process of fantasy play demonstrates a ***communicative circulation*** between source and manifestation. When the process results in something physically and sensorially tangible, visible, or audible, it provides immediate and perceivable feedback. This feedback triggers new thoughts, sensations, or emotions, which in turn are processed and manifested. It may lead to new thoughts in the person creating, but as long as the new "information" continues to be processed through play, additional material will be generated and expressed in some form or another. A circular process that constantly escalates and develops. In this way, what has been hidden within the child can be brought to the surface.

The Adult's Fantasy Play:
the approach of an artist

As an adult, fantasy play can be recognized in what is commonly referred to as an ***artistic process***. I create—through art, craftsmanship, or some other form of expression. I begin with a need to express myself, to manifest what exists within me through something external: the word, the colour, the form, the tone, and so on. To do this, I need to be in touch with the material—whether it be words, sounds, tones, musical intervals, colours, the body, or the physical substance—that will carry my expression.

Just as the child explores the possibilities of a material, I, as an adult, can adopt ***an exploratory approach*** to any material, even to materials as "close" as my own voice, body, or words. Even though the need for expression is the driving force, I must create a balance between input and output for *the communicative circulation between myself and the material* to emerge. I must, in a sense, listen to the material I am working with.

It is easy to get stuck in a limbo—experiencing creative block—when I remain *solely in an expressive state.* Habits, defence mechanisms, and an attachment to the familiar are some of the factors that can cause the artistic process to stagnate. There may also be fear of certain expressions, or fear of what I might discover in what I manifest.
What is missing is ***a courageous dialogue*** with the material.

231

To reopen the creative process, I must **re-establish communication between myself and the material.** I must begin to listen, set aside my need for expression for a moment, and wait for the material's "response". It is in the encounter with the material, in the balance between doing and listening, in the reciprocity, that playfulness can re-emerge. It may seem strange to listen to a "lifeless" material that does not speak, or to my own voice or movement—*as if they belonged to someone else.* But the secret lies precisely in this approach: **to relate to the material as if it is speaking to me—through the impressions it provides.** What else would I *interact* with?—*the interaction that is one of the keys to creativity.*

What speaks is my subconscious, "speaking through the material." Also present are the collective unconscious and the material's own qualities and properties. But most importantly: *what I hear is what I need to hear—if I have the courage to listen beyond what I want to hear.* This is the common denominator between children's imaginative play and the artistic process of adults — a playing or a process that gives me insights into myself as well as my relationship with the world around me.

When I strive for a dialogue with the material, something wonderful happens: the material itself *draws* me out of my comfort zone. Through this courageous dialogue, I allow the material to awaken unexpected aspects of myself—things I might not have chosen to manifest consciously. It may bring forth hidden content, undiscovered qualities, and unknown aspects of myself.

Habits, "darlings," comfort zones, and fears of the unknown must give way. The dialogue lifts me out of my limitations—both those I am aware of and those I have yet to recognize—and into a creative flow. The circular movement of fantasy play, between source and manifestation, has begun.

The way out of creative block or a lack of inspiration lies in this duality: *to listen inwardly as well as outwardly in the encounter with the material.* I must allow it to guide me forward and outward, into a creative movement *where something new can always emerge.*

As long as I engage in interactions and align myself with what the interaction requires, there are no limits to creation.

Playfulness has no end.

- *The Dramatic Play*

The Dramatic Play is about collaborative fantasy play and exists between Fantasy Play and Rule-Based Play

On one hand, it encompasses what Fantasy Play offers—the child's inner reality, which is processed and expressed—and on the other hand, it includes the need to share these expressions in community and interaction. Interaction with other participants adds new dimensions and depth to the play. *The presence of others, their personalities and traits, as well as their needs and motives for playing, serve*—just like the physical material in fantasy play—*as a catalyst, drawing out new, previously hidden aspects of oneself.*

The shared experience not only creates unique situations that foster a sense of belonging but also provides a space where strong emotions can be expressed: *fear, anger, excitement, joy, laughter, and intimacy.* In a safe group, a safe and allowing space, the community becomes a safety net where emotions and expressions, which in solitude might not dare to emerge, can now flourish. This safety net in collaborative play is also constituted by explicit or implicit play rules and guidelines. These rules function as a *fundamental structure or framework* that allows dramatic play to unfold freely. Structures may *include roles, status, specific relationships between roles, actions, and/or specific tasks (missions and goals).*

234

For the play to reach its optimal form, there must also be mutual acceptance of each other's ways of responding and being within the agreed framework. Here, *the ability to express and empathise is practised*—but now in relation to other people, which is something entirely different from merely relating to physical materials. Interaction with other individuals requires connection—an intentional engagement with those one is playing with. It is precisely in this connection with others that disorders and traumas can often arise. *However, it is also here that certain attachment disorders can begin to heal—given enough time.*

This is where *the capacity for empathy is founded*—the ability to feel with and understand another, to experience their way of being, feeling, and thinking. *Tolerance is also cultivated here*, even when it feels difficult to allow—for the sake of the flow of play. Tolerance for our differences in being and responding can trigger discomfort within us. *Learning to live with these personal inner discomforts—to remain with them without slipping into stress and losing presence—sharpens our ability to function socially.*

Social life thus becomes a field for co-creation—through play.

Adults: from "Playing around" to Authentic play—the Social Art

For this form of play, this approach to life, to continue into adulthood and be optimised, *attentiveness, generosity, and acceptance* are required.

- **Attentiveness** involves being receptive to others' expressions and needs.

- **Generosity** means sharing one's own ways of expression freely.

- **Acceptance** is about welcoming and embracing others' ways and choices of expression.

Here, the fundamental rules of improvisation are practised: never blocking what comes from another, but rather receiving it and making something of what is offered—during play as well as during life.

Normally we know the "social game" as something *inauthentic*, where individual differences, traits, and needs *do not fully have a place.* There is a lack of acceptance. However, *acceptance begins with ourselves in relation to ourselves.* The rejection of aspects in others, as is well known, stems from the rejection of an inner, private, and hidden conflict that one struggles to resolve. An old truth.

But the more I allow of what is truly me—my needs; what I feel, experience, and perceive; how I perform tasks; how my expressions take shape, how I move, how I sound, and so on— the easier it will be to extend acceptance to my surroundings. This new attitude towards oneself liberates one from falling into criticism and blockage of others.

One's approach, whether blocking or accepting, spreads to others, making it easier for them to adopt a more accepting stance towards themselves—and, in turn, towards others.

Then, the social game transforms into an increasingly *authentic social play*—in the best sense of the word.

Authentic, in the sense that the participant engages as a whole and integrated individual, affirming themselves and their needs.

Play, in the sense that the participant understands and adapts to the components of play: being empathetic (*present*) with co-players; engaging in communication (*interaction)*; and sensing within yourself how you need to play and contribute to the shared play (*your own dynamic*). "The social game" (*where you must play the role   with masks assigned to you*) thus evolves into *social creation*—where you are a co-creater.

The social art

Now, we can begin to speak *The social art*. An art where the "material" consists of human beings and the circumstances and situations at hand. There are rules that we—the people, the work teams, the friendships—have democratically chosen to adhere to. Rules that primarily create *safety,* rather than unease and prohibition (*dictatorship*); that primarily offer *opportunities*, rather than excluding unknown possibilities (*conservatism*); that primarily facilitate *creation,* rather than obstructing and causing stagnation and delays (*bureaucracy*). Good rules and frameworks are those that *enhance playfulness and creativity.* As soon as one notices that these are not thriving, ***the rules for co-creation should be changed***—always in the best pedagogical spirit.

The theatre of life

For over a hundred years, theatre has sought *authenticity in acting* (*Stanislavski, Copeau, Grotowski, Strasberg, Adler, Meisner, and many others*). Exercises and methods have been developed. The question has been: how can an actor be genuine on stage? How can an actor, despite portraying a completely different character—say, Hamlet—still be themselves, as deeply as possible? A paradox, perhaps?

Since ancient Greek times and the "*Dionysian festivals,*" theatre has been a stage for life's dramas. A fragment of life has been extracted from its context and condensed into a theatrical performance lasting a few hours. From the theatre phenomenon come expressions such as: *"you're just playing a role," "what role do I have in this?" "this is life's theatre," "you're just dramatising!"* and so on. We experience life as a drama— sometimes as *"pure comedy.*" We feel that we play different roles in different contexts. We sometimes perceive ourselves as creative, but more often—and especially when it comes to social life—we find ourselves merely following along. Too often, we feel like victims of life; that life tosses us around; sometimes things go up, sometimes down.

One thing is certain: we are not alone on the stage of life. There are fellow players, and circumstances. And we all carry our own background music (our film score), accompanying our every move.

But our first concern should not be how to escape (to another theatre stage, perhaps?). No, rather, it should be how to play our role in the drama we are placed in. And the answer to that question is unequivocal: t*o play authentically.* Or more accurately: to ***be authentic***. I almost hesitate to write it. It is so obvious that it feels silly to say. Easy to say, but hard to be. We all know that. But the premiere is tonight! No—it is now! The premiere is always now!

Yet, as mentioned, you are not alone on stage. And there are reassuring, agreed-upon guidelines. Listen to them, listen to your co-actors, and listen to everything that can be perceived on the stage (*the pre-play stage*). Start interacting (*interaction*) with what you choose to focus on (presence) while simultaneously sensing how you and your body want to engage (*dynamics*). Now, playfulness begins to flow, and together with the others on the stage of life, you begin to co-create *co-living*.

PART

4

The Playfulness
and Creativity
Troubleshooting

Note:

For the checklist below to be useful, it is essential that you have read and at least partially understood the foundational concepts of playfulness and creativity as outlined in Part 1.

This checklist offers a series of questions to turn to when something feels missing, progress halts, creative energy runs dry, or conflicts — internal or social — become entrenched. It applies to challenges in work, art, creativity, school, friendships, close relationships, or really, any aspect of life.

If I feel stuck in research, exploration, or when something loses its joy or meaning, this list helps identify what might be missing. Playfulness and creativity is delicate — if any of its foundational elements are absent, imbalance arises, leading to such difficulties.

troubleshooting

First, a very short, simple and quick checklist that you can learn by heart before I present more in-depth questions:

Quick-Check List to Ignite Playfulness and creativity

1. Am I interacting with someone or something?
   If not, start now!

2. Am I fully present in this interaction?
   If not, be present!

3. Am I stuck in what I expected or wished for?
   If so, let it go!

4. Are the dynamics balanced?

   o E.g. Am I lingering too long in one activity, focus, or dynamic, or am I rushing ahead too quickly? Pause, notice, and adjust!

   o E.g. Have I struck a pace that is neither too fast nor too slow to support my presence? Find the balance!

When all three — Presence, Connection, and Dynamics — are balanced, playfulness and creativity can flourish naturally.

- *The Pre-Play Stage*

The questions in the pre-play stage relate to ***Arriving, Perceiving, Receiving, and Accepting.***

1. Arriving / Settling - Grounding

Sense whether all of me has truly arrived at the place or situation I've stepped into. Am I present in my body? Can I feel its entirety? Have I settled into the emotional and mental currents within me?

The more fully I "am here," the more information I can absorb. It often involves, as the saying goes, "leaving your coat at the door" or "dusting off the road dirt." Even if I've been in this room before, every situation is, in fact, a new situation. Anything I fail to leave behind, anything I allow to linger, will act as a filter for my perception and experience of the new moment.

It is my responsibility—and indeed my joy—to make each situation a fresh one, to regard it with a sense of wonder.

I need not worry that this will leave me disoriented; my mind will be sharper, more open to new information.

The key question is:

Have I landed and am I entirely present in myself, here and now?
Am I grounded, centered, and rooted in myself?

2. Perceiving / Sensing—Listening

At this point, I am prepared to gather information through all my senses. I make a conscious effort to notice whether I am already reflecting on the information I am receiving, and instead, I strive simply to remain present with the sensory impressions themselves. In this phase, I am not concerned with controlling the situation, and therefore, I need not engage in reflection or form judgments.

The key question is:
Am I ready and open to fully embrace the reality as it exists, here and now, without reservation?

3. Receiving / Absorbing—Embracing

Internally affirming an unreserved "Yes!" to the incoming information is both fundamental and vital. At this stage, my role is not to intervene or contribute; rather, I must first comprehend the information inwardly — to perceive it. This may not always involve intellectual understanding; often, true comprehension arises later, when I step back and reflect on the experience retrospectively.

At times, this understanding is simply an emotional or sensory acceptance of what is entering my awareness. What might **obstruct** this process are the conscious or, more frequently, unconscious prejudices, decisions, and conclusions regarding what is deemed permissible or possible. These mechanisms — often powerful (the less conscious, the more forcefully they assert themselves) — act as filters, blocking certain aspects of reality from my awareness.
The remedy lies in heightening my presence and refraining from intervening until the interaction between myself and the information unfolds naturally. Recognising these internal barriers can lead to a heightened awareness.

The key question is:
Are there prejudices, discriminations, decisions, values, conclusions, fears, or exclusions that are impeding my perception, which need to be cleared away?

4. Accepting / Being—Resting Awake

By first acknowledging, accepting, and embracing both my internal and external realities, I grant myself the ability to simply "be" with them. Only at this point can I truly engage with the situation at hand.

The key question is:
Can I be with what is, or is there something within me that I am still resisting?

Reflecting on the four pre-play steps — Arriving, Perceiving, Receiving, and Accepting — forms the basis for cultivating or restoring playfulness and creativity. This phase opens the door to creativity, joy, and harmony in relationships, work, or life in general.

- The Core Elements of Playfulness

The three core elements of playfulness — **Interactivity, Presence and Dynamics** — are deeply interwoven, revolving around one another. To manage them consciously and simultaneously is an art, akin to juggling. The questions must flow effortlessly amongst these spheres in the present moment.

For **Presence**, ask:

- Has my presence diminished because I:

  o   Have not clarified the focus of my attention?

  o   Have become distracted and lost focus on the chosen object?

For **Interactivity**, ask:

- Has my interactivity faltered because I:

  o   Lost contact?

  o   Lost Reciprocity?

  o   Blocked impulses or information?

  o   Failed to let them resonate within me?

troubleshooting

For **Dynamics**, ask:

- Have I failed to honour my personal dynamics regarding:

  ○ Clearly ending or beginning actions (On/Off)?

  ○ Challenging my limits too little or too much (Wildness/Stillness)?

  ○ Navigating chaos or structuring order (Chaos/Structure)?

Tip: If **Interactivity** falters, review both **Presence** and **Dynamics**. Without one, the other two cannot thrive.

_____

- *Obstructive Patterns*

When energy wanes or interaction feels stilted, consider whether any of these blocking patterns are at play:

1. **Expectations and Wishes**

2. **Projections and Applications**

3. **Conclusions and Viewpoints**

4. **Judgements and Opinions**

5. **Stagnant Decisions**

6. **Stagnant Separations**

7. **Fixed Relating**

The first four are tied to *thought and emotion*, distancing you from the present reality.

- **Expectations and Wishes**: Create resistance to what is.

- **Projections**: Distort reality by imposing prior experiences.

- **Conclusions and Viewpoints**: Narrow possibilities by fixed perspectives.

- **Judgements**: Emotionally reinforce disconnection.

The latter three operate within the realm of will, directly limiting engagement with the present.

- **Stagnant Decisions**: Restrict future possibilities by clinging to fixed stances.

- **Stagnant Separations**: Filter out aspects of reality before they reach awareness.

- **Fixed Relating**: Introduces irrelevant biases and actions into the present.

Explanation

- When *expectations and desires* for something different arise, they block your ability to connect with what is, rendering it difficult to handle.

- If you *project or impose* prior experiences or ideas onto what actually is, the information that reaches you becomes distorted.

Conclusions and viewpoints place you in a reflective position, confined to a specific perspective, shutting out more expansive possibilities. Reflection itself requires—and creates—distance. This distance severs your connection.

- Similarly, ***judgements and opinions*** function in much the same way, though their tone is more emotional.

- A ***stagnant decision*** is a fixed stance taken toward what is and what might be. Certain things *"must not, under any circumstance, happen or appear"* in a particular way. It is as though a decision has been etched into the fabric of your being, destined to govern the rest of your life. In turn, the possibilities for what might unfold are sharply limited.

- ***Stagnant separations*** function as rigid filters, pre-emptively dividing one thing from another. These filters isolate parts of reality before they even reach awareness. Certain aspects of reality fail to surface in your consciousness, having already been sifted out in the journey between perception and understanding. As a result, the opportunities for *new* encounters and fresh points of contact become restricted.

- ***Fixed relating*** involves the relationships I have constructed towards someone or something. It might concern a specific individual, a category such as gender or ethnicity, or even an object like the colour red or an activity like dance. Relating, by its very nature, creates a distance from that which I wish to be fully present with. This unintended distancing introduces irrelevant actions and judgements into what is unfolding here and now.

In short, these obstructive patterns ensure that "nothing new takes place under the sun." However, since every new encounter and every interaction carries within it the potential for future possibilities, a conflict with reality arises, hindering the development of these opportunities.

This conflict may occur within the thinking, creative, and exploratory individual, or it may manifest in the social sphere. Either way, it inhibits the future, the new, the fresh, and the playful.

There is no inherent flaw in relationships, conclusions, desires, or judgments. However, when these take control instead of playfulness and creativity themselves, when they have stagnated and lost their inner flexibility, and particularly when they fall outside your awareness, allowing their limiting influence to take charge, that is when creativity and life are buried — far too young.

As you can understand, this is about examining oneself, taking the time to reflect, and discovering these otherwise hidden behavioural patterns. Each pattern is a part of our personality and will remain so until it is uncovered and dissolved. And as long as these patterns are left unaddressed, they will be an obstacle to your creativity and playful approach to life.

- *Additional Reflections*

- A lack of **Interaction** may stem from an absence of a conscious decision to be Present or from the need to shift towards another activity (**Dynamics**).

- A lack of **Presence** might arise from an unwillingness to engage with what is at hand. In such cases, an updated decision or a change of direction (**Dynamics**) is required, or perhaps a greater allowance for **your own resonance** to emerge.

- You experience **Flow** in the interaction, yet it is constantly *disrupted* by external factors. Check the **Contact** and **Reciprocity** components of the interaction.

- You feel **Connected**, but you become fatigued *(true playfulness is never exhausting)*. Have you forgotten to honour your personal **Dynamics**? Perhaps it's time to shift activities?

- You feel **Present**, yet no positive emotions arise *(playfulness always brings positive emotions*)*. Are you fully aware of what you are interacting with and of what this interaction expects of you?

- You sense the freedom to change activities at will, and you do, yet you feel lonely *(play always fosters a sense of togetherness—even when you are alone)*. Are you truly committing enough and allowing your resonance to deepen? Do you dare to let yourself go for a while, to become mutual with others or with the moment? Do you have the courage to stay Present?

Coda: Afterglow

My hope is that you, dear reader, will increasingly find your own playfulness and awaken your creativity, allowing it to fill and permeate every aspect of life that you encounter. Life will be filled with you—your presence, your transformation and re-creation of what life offers you. And to the extent that you have discovered true playfulness, you will also find many playmates and co-creators of the life you hold in your hands.

I hope you give yourself many opportunities to practice Presence, Interaction, Dynamics and Intuition—both alone and together. You will find your ways. You will find your path.

Wishing you joy and good fortune!

Warm regards,

Kefas, Mölnbo in April 2025

Literature list

Albert, David H	And the Skylarks sings with Me - adventures in homeschooling and community-based education
Bateson, Patrik; Martin ,Paul	Play, Playfulness, Creativity and Innovation
Bergström, Matti	Barnet—den Sista Slaven
Bergström, Matti	Svarta och Vita Lekar—Kaos och Ordning i hjärnan, om det lekande barnet
Bogart, Anne; Landau, Tina	The Viewpoint Book—A practical Guide to Viewpoints and Composition
Brown Stuart L	Discovering the Importance of Play through Personal Histories and Brain Images
Brown, Stuart L	Consequences of Play Deprivation
Brown, L Stuart	Play—How it shapes the brain, opens the imagination, and invigorates the soul
Burghardt, Gordon M	The Genesis of Animal Play—Testing the Limits
Cameron, Julia	The Artist's Way
Csikszentmihalyi, Mihaly	Flow: the Psychology of optimal Experience
Donaldson, Fred	Playing by Heart
Frankl, Viktor	Man's Search for Meaning
Gray Peter	The Decline of Play and the Rise of Psychopathology in Children and Adolescents

Gray Peter	The Role of Play in the Development of Social and Emotional Competence
Gray, Peter	Free to Learn—Why unleashing the instinct to play will make our children happier, more self-reliant and better students for life
Gray, Peter	The End of Play – Why Kids Need Unstructured Time (Youtube)
Greenberg, Daniel	A place to Grow—The Culture of Sudbury Valley School
Greenberg, Daniel	Free at Last—The Sudbury Valley School
Greenberg, Daniel; Sadofsky, Mimsy	Starting a Sudbury School—A Summary of the Experiences of Fifteen Start-up Groups
Hodge, Alison (edit)	Twentieth Century Actor Training
Huber, Mike	Embracing Rough-and-Tumble-play
Huizinga, Johan	Homo Ludens—A study of the play-element in culture
Jackins, Harvey	The Human Side of Human Beings: the Theory of Re-evaluation Counselling
Jackins, Harvey	The Human Situation
Jensen, Mikael	Lekteorier
Johnstone, Keith	Impro
Juul, Jesper	Your competent child: Toward a new Paradigm in Parenting and Education
Juul, Jesper	Family Life: the most important Values for Living together and Raising Children
Kischnick, Rudolf; van Haren, Wil	Childs Play book 1 & 2—Games for Life

Koritz, Rebecka   En Skola från Scratch

Kuhfuß, Werner   Das Wasser bildet seine Ufer selbst—Wie
                                                   soziales Leben unter Kindern entsteht.

Kuhfuß, Werner   Evolution genom lek: nya Vägar i
                                                   Behandlingen av Barn i behov av
                                                   Kroppslig och Själslig Vård

Levine, Peter   In an Unspoken Voice

May, Rollo   The Courage to Create

McDonalds, Kerry   Unschooled—Raising Curious,
                                                   Well-Educated Children Outside the
                                                   Conventional Classroom

Miller, Alice   The Drama of the Gifted Child
                                                   —The Search for the True Self

Panksepp, Jaak   The Importance of Play—an Interview

Panksepp, Jaak   Can PLAY Diminish ADHD and Facilitate
                                                   the Construction of the Social Brain?

Pellegrini; Smith (edit)   The Nature of Play—Great Apes and
                                                   Humans

Robinson, Ken; Aronica, Lou   Creative Schools—The Grassroots
                                                   Revolution That's Transforming Education

Robinson, Ken   Do Schools Kill Creativity?
                                                   — TED Talk

Robinson, Ken   Bring on the Learning Revolution
                                                   — TED Talk

Schiller, Friedrich   On the Aesthetic Education of Man

Staniewski, Wlodomierz; Hodge Allison   Hidden Territories
                                                   —The Theatre of Gardzienice

Wang, Stephen

An Acrobat of the Heart—A physical Approach to Acting Inspired by the Work of Jerzy Grotowski

Whitbread, David

The Importance of Play—A Report on the Value of Children's Play with a Series of Policy Recommendations

Workshops in playfulness—and everything connected to it—are led by Kefas Berlin and can be booked by schools, training centres, institutions, conferences, or companies seeking to enhance creativity, innovation, and playfulness. Each workshop is carefully tailored to the group's specific needs and real-life questions.

Play and playfulness have also proven to be powerful tools in resolving socially challenging situations—whether in schools, workplaces, or teams struggling with internal conflict, poor communication, or a lack of innovation. Decades of experience with such interventions have shown great success. I'm happy to help.

Contact Kefas Berlin:
theliberatedvoice@gmail.com

For open workshops and more:
www.kefasberlin.se

Your notes

Your notes

Your notes

Your notes

Your notes

Your notes